ETHICS IN BUSINESS

ETHICS IN BUSINESS

Faith at Work

James M. Childs Jr.

FORTRESS PRESS
MINNEAPOLIS

To Linda

ETHICS IN BUSINESS
Faith at Work

Cover illustration: *Paper Disc to Collect Dust*, James Rosenquist, 1984, 8″ x 6¼″, one-color aquatint/etching, collection of James Rosenquist, copyright © 1995 James Rosenquist/Licensed by VAGA, New York, NY. Used by Permission.

Cover and text design: Joseph Bonyata

Library of Congress Cataloging-in-Publication Data

Childs, James M., 1939-
    Ethics in business : faith at work / James M. Childs Jr.
        p.   cm.
    Includes bibliographical references and index.
    ISBN 0-8006-2908-6 (alk. paper)
    1. Business ethics. 2. Business—Religious aspects—Christianity.
3. Christian ethics. I. Title.
HF5387.C48 1995
241´.624—dc20   95-19154
                                                      CIP

The paper used in this publication meets the minimum requirements of American National Standard for Information Sciences—Permanence of Paper for Printed Library Materials, ANSI Z329.4-1984.

Manufactured in the U.S.A..   AF 1-2908
99   98   97   2   3   4   5   6   7   8   9   10

CONTENTS

PREFACE

Is it possible to function successfully in business and maintain one's ethical integrity as a Christian? Is there a genuine Christian vocation for those in business? Are there special Christian insights on ethical issues such as whistle-blowing, affirmative action, or environmental responsibility? How can I make my Christian witness heard and appreciated in the secular world of business? How is it possible for Christianity or any other religious faith to have much impact on the ethics of business in a world as pluralistic as ours?

This book is meant for people who struggle with these questions or for whom these questions strike a responsive chord and that point to issues of importance today.

I want to offer such persons an encouragement and, I hope, a helpful resource in dealing with these questions and the issues they involve.

The foremost encouragement comes from the promises of God in Jesus Christ which affirm us and empower us in our aspirations to faithful witness. These promises are always at the vital center of our discussion. There are, however, other encouragements as well. Our contemporary culture, despite its baffling pluralism and seeming loss of moral consensus, provides Christians and the Christian community with some important new avenues of witness. The avenues I have in mind are the various possibilities of participating in ethical dialogue, both in the context of business and among the stakeholders of business in the larger society. The process of dialogue, which is at the strategic center of the discussion that follows, opens us up to one another in our diversity and enables us to speak with integrity out of the particular perspectives of our experience and our faith. I hope to show that diversity can foster that kind of dialogue. It does so by forcing us to deal with one another's ethical vision in its cultural and religious particularity rather than imagining that we can all discourse together in some neutral language of rationality.

There is further encouragement in the rising tide of ethical concern among business leaders in our day. My numerous personal contacts confirmed this interest and provided examples of individuals who are working hard at the blend of faith and life. Personal encounters of this sort and the burgeoning literature of business ethics also give us helpful paradigms of organizations whose ethical sensibilities are creating a climate congenial to Christian participation.

Finally, there is encouragement in the willingness of increasing numbers of church, educational, and business and professional leaders to interact on issues of ethical business. There is in this willingness a growing recognition that the impact of national and global business on the quality of individual life and the common good is incalculable.

One such organization is the Council for Ethics in Economics in Columbus, Ohio. The nature and activities of the council are discussed briefly in the book itself. For now, as a member of the council who has been with it since its inception, I simply want to acknowledge that the contacts I have had with business and professional leaders, as well as other church leaders and educators, have been among the most enriching in my experience. The fourteen years I have participated in the council's activities have in large measure provided the impetus for the writing of this book. I am particularly grateful to Dr. Paul Minus, the president of the Council for Ethics in Economics, for his collegiality, his encouragement, and his helpful comments on the manuscript.

I am grateful to President Dennis Anderson and the board of directors of Trinity Lutheran Seminary for the recent sabbatical, during which much of the research and writing was done. I am also grateful to Lutheran Brotherhood and Aid Association for Lutherans, each of whose generous grants to faculty development provided necessary support to various phases of my research.

Thanks are due to a variety of anonymous witnesses whose shared comments found their way into the text and whose encouragement for the project helped to keep me going. I am deeply appreciative of the helpful counsel of Michael Perry and James Gustafson at the critical beginning stages of shaping my ideas. I credit them for their collegiality and insightful help and excuse them from any liability for the shortcomings of this work.

I want to extend my thanks to Dean Ron Volpe of the Capital University Graduate School of Administration for giving me the opportunity to teach the course in Business and Society for the M.B.A. program at Capital. I am grateful also for the help and assistance in that enterprise from my colleague and collaborator in that course, Prof. Michael Distelhorst of the Capital University Law and Graduate Center. Participation in that course enabled me to test and develop some of my ideas as the manuscript was nearing its completion.

I have enjoyed working with Michael West at Fortress Press. I thank him for his patience and encouragement, and for the interest he has taken in my work.

A large debt of gratitude goes to Sue Stover, my administrative assistant, who not only has rendered invaluable assistance in the preparation of the manuscript but also was a partner in effectively organizing the activities of our office and enabling me to find the energy and the time to complete this writing project.

Finally, in this enterprise as in all of my work, I am thankful to and for my wife, Linda, and my whole family for providing that sustaining ground of love on which we all need to stand if we are to do our work with a complete sense of meaning and enthusiasm.

1

BRIDGING THE

SHAREABILITY GAP

aith shapes ethical business practice. Actions and decisions need to be responsible to all the stakeholders. For example, in banking, you don't sell someone a product they don't need or shouldn't buy just because you can sell it and it will increase your numbers. At the same time, if you discontinue an unprofitable product, you have to think about how to take care of those left in the lurch who need a product like the one you're dropping. Prioritize relationships over numbers and the numbers will come."

Stan thought for a moment and then went on. "Another way I see my Christian ethics expressed in my business practice is when I try in my community relations responsibilities to help make banking services responsive to community needs. When the local community came to the bank protesting that they needed more loans and other services in their area, I listened. I didn't try to fight them or ignore them. Together we worked out a strategy that was realistic; the bank helped them as much as possible, and they recognized and respected the financial realities the bank had to work with. I think my efforts to build relationships with the community were a contribution I made as a Christian. It stands in contrast to the kind of bad mentality that always sees the other party in a dispute as the enemy who has to be undermined or discredited."

"It sounds to me like your faith as a Christian plays a big role in your daily work life," I said. "Has the church been a help to you in that regard? A great many businesspeople feel that the church has not paid much attention to the faith-life connection."

"It is probably true that the church doesn't fully appreciate the needs of people in the business world, but," he added with great emphasis, "the church has endorsed my vocation in life; what I do has meaning." Stan went on to say with equal emphasis that the church needs to continue to support and encourage people in a sense of "vocation" that gives meaning and direction to their life and work.

The name Stan is fictitious, but the person is real. This brief exchange from a longer conversation we had serves to introduce the project of this book. It helps us to see both the needs and the possibilities for relating Christian faith and ethics to business. It grounds that effort in the lives of real people. We shall return to these points soon.

BUSINESS ETHICS: A GROWING CONCERN

In recent years business ethics has become a growing concern in two senses of the word *concern*: a worry and a business.

The worrisome state of standards of ethical practice in business has been so much in the public eye that it hardly needs discussion. James W. Kuhn and Donald W. Shriver Jr. begin their book on business ethics with this telling observation: "Over the past decade, and with increasing frequency, public commentators have accused business managers of unethical doings and an alarming lack of morality in the conduct of their firms' affairs. The business press, regular newspapers, and television news programs regularly report the latest account of the low standards of behavior in high corporate offices."[1]

Kuhn and Shriver go on to say that business has responded to this public indictment in a variety of ways. To some extent this response has been defensive. However, for a significant number of corporations, public concern for business ethics has provided the occasion for new efforts to make ethical consciousness an integral part of the corporate culture through managerial leadership, the establishment of standards and practices, and the development of ethics training programs.[2] One of my colleagues has even described this renewal of ethical consciousness in business as a "movement of conscience" among key leaders in American business.

The Business Roundtable, in its 1988 report *Corporate Ethics: A Prime Business Asset,* gives us a picture of industry mobilizing to meet the demands of sound business ethics, which the report characterizes as "one of the most challenging issues confronting the corporate community in this era."[3] As the title suggests, the conclusion reached by the study is that corporate ethics is essential to good business, indeed, even to survival.[4] The authors state further: "The corporate community should continue to refine and renew efforts to improve performance and manage change effectively through programs in corporate ethics."[5]

Clearly, many companies are taking positive steps to meet the challenge of business ethics in our time. The pages ahead examine some of them. Still the concern remains. Just today, as I write these words, I remember the comment made this morning at an ethics discussion group of local human resources executives. One of those present expressed surprise at how few were attending these sessions, given the fact that ethical questions pervade every aspect of business life from hiring and marketing to health care and benefits.

With people more and more worried about promoting good business ethics, it is not surprising to find business ethics becoming a growing industry or business in its own right. Ethics consulting firms, videos, journals, books, and academic programs in business ethics have proliferated at a remarkable speed.

On the theoretical level, the development of business ethics has been dominated by moral philosophy and moral philosophers who often incorporate elements of moral development theory drawn from psychology. A recent survey of the most frequently used business ethics textbooks in business school courses gives clear evidence of this dominant orientation.[6] An analysis by the respected business ethicist Frida Furman of how business ethics courses are taught reveals an overwhelming disposition among business ethicists to work out of traditional philosophical categories of ethical reasoning.[7] Many of the same teachers have also become busy consultants to businesses and produced books and videos, thereby multiplying the influence of their approach.

The predominant reliance on the rational argumentation of philosophy, coupled with the contributions of the behavioral sciences, to give an account of how morality works and should be practiced is typical of a long tradition of trust in reason and empirical research that has held sway for nearly three hundred years. This is the legacy of the Enlightenment. Since the dawn of that era in the seventeenth century, we have witnessed a steady increase in secularization of our Western world. At the core of modern secularity is the conviction that we are emancipated from the superstitions and taboos of religion and supernaturalism and free to pursue the good of humankind under the guidance of our own best thought.

In all fields of human endeavor, reason and objectivity have become the hallmark of how we operate in modern, Western, secular culture. In the area of public policy debate and formation, for example, we have insisted upon reasoned and objective argumentation in the belief that that method alone can lead us to standards and policies that are universally understood and accepted.

The business community has drunk as deeply from these ideological wells as any other institution of our society. Business reflects the values of the larger culture in which it operates.[8] In the 1970s psychoanalyst Michael Maccoby did a study of five hundred corporate managers. He concluded that "by schooling and experience, managers of large American corporations are trained to take a 'detached,' rational-objective view of the corporation's internal and external problems."[9] It would seem, on the face of it, then, that business ethics based on reasoned argument and empirical research would be more acceptable than, for example, an ethical system rooted in religious convictions or cultural traditions. We will need to test that assumption.

THE LIMITS OF REASON

I shall say more later about the tradition of rationalism in our society and the way it has influenced our ethics. For now, it is sufficient to note briefly that there are limits to reason's ability to lead us to moral consensus, at least as regards the concept of reason with which we have been operating in the modern era.

Today we realize that reason is not only incapable of achieving consensus in ethics but also not always able to construct arguments that everyone will readily understand. What is convincing to one on the basis of "sound reason" may be unconvincing to another or even strange and hard to understand. There is growing evidence that people do not all think the same way, by which I do not mean "have the same opinion"; I mean the way they go about thinking about things is different, depending on their life histories. Therefore, even our most carefully reasoned arguments are in some significant way influenced by the particular histories we have lived rather than purely objective.

Psychologist Anne Wilson Schaef has argued persuasively that men and women have different versions of reality, which govern their thought. Similarly, members of ethnic groups have a view of the world that is shaped by the group's particular history. Different outlooks mean basically different patterns of thinking.[10] It is an indication of the importance of this insight to business that it is hard to pick up a recent business ethics text without finding a respectful discussion of Carol Gilligan's *In a Different Voice*. Her research on the moral development of women, as contrasted to similar research with men, shows a tendency for women to think ethically in terms of relationships rather than rules or principles; caring and responsibility are key ethical constructs reflecting the sensibilities developed by women out of the particular features of their experience.[11] As greater numbers of women enter management, it is essential that business leadership gains an appreciation of the realities that research like Gilligan's uncovers.

Whether it is women leading us to a new understanding of the importance of relationships in our approach to business ethics or, to give another example, Native Americans schooling us in a deeper sense of the sacredness of the natural environment, the idea that we have a neutral language of reason, unalloyed by the particularities of social and cultural experience, that can lead us to a moral consensus does not wash in our pluralistic society. Eric Mount Jr. has summarized these points:

> Recourse to human "rationality" and some universally acknowledged morality offers limited help for several reasons. The first is the elusiveness of the content of this morality that all rational beings supposedly know and espouse. What seems perfectly rational to most people in Iran or China may not always seem so to most people in the United States. We have lived such different stories that we often make sense of things differently. Even within our own country, it becomes more and more questionable to assume immersion in a common story. The vaunted voice of reason is heard differently by people from different backgrounds with different makeups functioning in different institutional settings.[12]

These comments alert us to the fact that not only will our eventual discussion of ethics in business have to deal with the impact of pluralism on the tradition of rationalism in terms of our own society, but also we will have to put international pluralism on our agenda, especially given the increasingly global character of business.

THE FAITH CONNECTION

Moving beyond the question of the adequacy of rational grounds for ethical consensus in business and other arenas of moral discussion, we simply need to observe, on the basis of what has just been said, that managers and others engaged in business bring with them the values and principles expressive of whatever history or story or belief system has shaped their lives and focused their moral visions. Indeed, the business ethicist Laura L. Nash has defined business ethics in a way that embodies this virtual truism: "Business ethics is the study of how personal moral norms apply to the activities and goals of commercial enterprise. It is not a separate moral standard, but the study of how the business context poses its own unique problems for the moral person who acts as an agent of this system."[13]

The fact of the matter is that what many people in business bring with them to the job is a personal moral standard influenced not only by their particular cultural histories but also deeply rooted in religious faith. The opening excerpt from my conversation with Stan offers prima facie evidence of that fact. Stan's comments on connecting faith and ethics on the job are echoed by a number of businesspeople. Some even have the opportunity to express the connection overtly. One former chief executive officer (CEO) told me how it was not unusual for him or other members of his management team to commend a certain decision on an ethical problem by saying, "It is the Christian thing to do."

The evidence of people's attempts to relate faith to business ethics in the workplace is more than anecdotal. A recent questionnaire surveying the interests of members of the Council for Ethics in Economics in Columbus, Ohio, asked: "How do you view the role of your personal religious belief and heritage as you make business decisions?" Virtually all the businesspeople responding circled "very important." This was just a small survey for the purposes of program planning, but a sizeable study by the Center for Ethics and Corporate Policy in Chicago, the "Congregations and Business Life Project," provides considerable evidence of people struggling in earnest to integrate faith and daily work and expressing a keen desire for more assistance in their struggles.[14]

William E. Diehl has written extensively about businesspeople making the connections between faith and life and, in so doing, has tapped into a deep vein of interest. In his latest book, *The Monday Connection,* he describes ethics as one of the ministries of the laity in daily life.[15] However, as both Diehl's work and the Center for Ethics and Corporate Policy study suggest, making the connection between faith and ethics in the sphere of work is not always easy. Among the manifold ministries of congregational life, this area of need appears to be generally underserved. The former CEO whose management team spoke openly of ethical decisions as "the Christian thing to do" was probably having an unusual experience.

THE SHAREABILITY GAP

The application of ethical values and principles in their explicitly faith-related form in the affairs of business is often frustrated by a number of conditions. There may be more than the five I can identify, but they should be sufficient to characterize the situation we need to address.

1. In our secular world the conviction lingers that objective reason can lead us to moral truth along a path of neutrality.
Despite the fact that we are beginning to understand and appreciate the limits of rationalism, the legacy of secular liberalism and its concern to purge anything that might be perceived as a sectarian influence in business and public affairs is still very much with us as a part of our Enlightenment heritage.[16]

Not long ago I was engaged in a workshop on biblical faith and business ethics. An effort was being made to find helpful resources for business ethics in the Bible and to relate them to real-life situations. An executive of a large corporation in my discussion group related what he believed was a significant ethical question he would face when reporting to the senior management team in the coming week. When asked by another in the group how he felt the discussion we were having on biblical ethics might help him deal with this matter, he responded that, if he were to tell the management team that certain decisions should be considered in terms of their compatibility with biblical standards, he would be laughed out of the room. In most business discussions, certainly, a flat-footed, direct appeal to the Bible *would* seem odd. However, the larger point lurking in his comment is that, when it comes to institutional patterns of ethical deliberation, there is an accepted language of reasoned argument. Religious considerations may be operating within individuals' consciences, but the moral insights they evoke need to be translated into a neutral vocabulary.

2. A tendency to equate Christian ethical ideals with a few commonly held principles short-circuits more probing moral reflection.
The majority of the businesspeople I talked with in preparation for this book indicated to me that they were fortunate in never really being confronted with a serious moral dilemma on the job. It appears they meant they had been spared the more blatant challenges, such as being offered a bribe or being tempted to falsify reports. This reaction suggests that matters of serious ethical consequence are in people's thinking normally confined to the avoidance of behavior that violates common norms against stealing, cheating, lying, and harming others directly. In a society such as ours with a residual belief that our ethos is Judeo-Christian, it is for many but a short step from this mind-set to the assumption that such common norms and Christian ethical principles are basically identical. The tension between moral principles of faith life and work life is therefore diminished.

There is, of course, some truth to this assumption. Certainly it is arguable, for example, that the Ten Commandments have exerted considerable influence in establishing a few basic dos and don'ts that are important to the common good. It is of even greater importance to the common good for Christians and non-Christians alike to avoid and discourage actions that are a clear transgression of these rules. Nonetheless, the Christian ethical tradition is too rich in texture to be encompassed by a few generally accepted principles, standing alone without the extensive interpretation and elaboration the church has given them historically. Furthermore, the ethical issues that emerge when business life is analyzed from a Christian perspective are often subtler and pervade the entire structure of an organization rather than being confined to individual acts. Concentration on the obvious in principle and behavior can lead to a false sense of satisfaction and we may close our eyes to discoveries that our faith perspective might initiate.

I suppose it is a matter of not seeing the forest for the trees. Some of the most important contributions of faith to business life and ethics can easily be missed, contributions like those alluded to by Jack Mahoney, director of the Business Ethics Research Centre in London:

> The challenging and comprehensive contribution of Christianity to the ethical conduct of business is not the delivery of a series of arbitrary moral injunctions. It is an exploring within the realm of business of the practical consequences of those beliefs about God and humanity which Christians hold as their distinctive way of interpreting and construing human existence. It unashamedly asks ultimate questions about the purpose of life and of human society, and about the intrinsic purpose of business as one among many expressions of social relationships and activities. It also claims to offer answers to such questions in ways which do not just satisfy intellectual curiosity, but which have...behavioral implications for business activity at all levels.[17]

3. Among many Christians there remains a long-standing dualistic assumption that spiritual life and business life belong to separate worlds.
The separation of Sunday and Monday has been railed against in pulpits for as long as anybody can remember. Yet those who represent Sunday and those who represent Monday, with relatively few exceptions, have both done good jobs at keeping the separation in place.

Certainly business has often created an environment in which keeping personal, religious, and ethical values separate from operative values at work is essential to survival. We already touched upon one aspect of this in discussing the first source of frustration in applying faith to business. Robert Jackall, a sociologist, has done a well-known study of corporate life on the basis of his intimate long-term relationships with three different companies. His *Moral Mazes: The World of Corporate Managers* portrays corporate life as a bureaucratic patrimony in which expediency encourages the ambitious manager to divorce personal principles from the demands and expectations of success in the corporation: "The manager alert to expediency sees his bureaucratic world through a lens that might seem blurred to those outside the corporation and even to some inside who are unable to rid themselves of encumbering perspectives from other areas of their lives. It is a lens, however, that enables him to bring into exact focus the rules and relationships of his immediate world."[18]

Some critics of Jackall's work see it as overly harsh and pessimistic. Others see it as quite accurate. No one denies he has a hold on some important insights. These insights are echoed in part by a colleague of mine on a university business school faculty. When I asked him what the key moral issue is for businesspeople, he answered without hesitation,

"The reintegration of the self and values in the workplace." He was referring to the urgent need to overcome the pervasive and debilitating dualism that Jackall describes so poignantly. For Christians who are not so sure it ought to be that way, such compartmentalization of life is vexing. One executive spoke to me enthusiastically of the businesspersons' prayer breakfasts the mayor held in the large city where he works. "It was so exciting," he said, "to witness business leaders talking to one another about matters of faith; it was very freeing." The intimation, of course, is that it takes just such an event to free up people for connecting faith and life; it is not what normally happens.

If business traditions sometimes serve to frustrate the integration of one's personal spiritual life and values with one's life on the job, there is evidence that the church has not been as helpful as it might be in assisting people with that need. In George Gallup Jr.'s 1988 study of the unchurched American, he came to the conclusion that churches and synagogues could still reach these people if they were attentive to unmet needs among them in ways that they have not been attentive in the past. Most interesting for our purposes is his admonition to start reaching out to "those in business and the professions—businessmen, doctors, lawyers, and others who must constantly make ethical judgments, sometimes life-or-death decisions. These people are in great need of spiritual nourishment, but often are not receiving it."[19] This conviction is echoed by the conclusions of the Chicago study mentioned earlier:

> First, work issues and concerns should be addressed more frequently and deeply within the life of congregations. While many people affirm a link between faith and work, their understanding of that link is vague. Congregations can provide opportunities for members to share and discuss the concrete ethical dilemmas and dimensions of their work....The low level of congregational support reported by the respondents indicates that there is much room for improvement in this area.[20]

The shortcomings of the churches in helping people integrate faith and ethics in business life are deserving of mention as a separate point.

4. The church has often been hostile in its attitude toward business and has tended to neglect addressing the specific daily needs of those in business.
Years ago the makers of Morton Salt ran a number of radio jingles as part of their advertising campaign. I have a vivid memory of one in particular because I was a parish pastor and preacher at the time: "No one finds fault like a preacher finds fault. And no salt salts like Morton Salt salts." If that stereotype of preachers as people whose main talent is faultfinding is common and unfair, businesspeople can be forgiven if they hold to it.

Spokespersons for the church have often been highly critical of business in alienating ways that make many people in business feel that the church is their adversary and not their friend.

William E. Diehl takes issue with church leaders who speak "prophet- ically" but without understanding the problems of business ethics. They may be too quick to label an instance of wrongdoing by a company as "corporate greed."[21] Such labels are inflammatory and can easily be unfair. As David A. Krueger has observed in a recent *Christian Century* article, "It is not helpful, for instance, for the manager to hear the preacher offer wholesale denunciation of workforce reductions and plant closings as a symptom of corporate greed and the triumph of profits over people. Causal factors are rarely so simplistic."[22]

Many business practitioners would say that maintaining an image of integrity in the public eye is tough enough without having the church take potshots as well. Beyond the bad jokes about "business ethics" being a contradiction in terms, there is still a lingering suspicion about the sort of character it really takes to be successful in business. Laura L. Nash observes that we seldom make business figures our cultural heroes. It is much easier to idealize the courage of the tireless doctor, the crusading lawyer, or the teacher dedicated to truth than it is to lionize a corporate executive "nobly making money."[23] In this regard, she quotes former Ford Motor Company chairman Philip Caldwell's complaint that too many people equate being in business with being greedy and dishonest.[24]

5. Businesspeople often operate with a stereotype of the church as out of touch with the "real world" and incapable of understanding that world.
If elements of the church have unfairly stereotyped business, then the reverse has also been true. A goodly number of the business folks I talked with about my research for this book expressed satisfaction at the prospect that seminarians might be among those reading it (at least the ones who have to because they are in my class) because, they offered, seminary education is often out of touch with the world. A course in business ethics and a book on the subject that brought theology into con- tact with the real-life thoughts and problems of businesspeople struggling with on-the-job ethics would certainly be a step in the right direction.

One executive of a brokerage firm made a comment about the church and business ethics that continues to stand out in my memory. "The church," he said, "talks in terms of absolutes. But we deal with compro- mise on an hourly basis." He went on to demur and say that he was sure his impression was probably not true and somewhat unfair. Be that as it may, it focuses sharply on the distance many businesspeople feel between the church and their lives. The Chicago study discovered that church members, while appreciating pastoral care and counseling for many circumstances of life, ranked it low for work-related concerns. The study speculates that this ranking is low, perhaps, because businesspeople do not believe that pastors understand and appreciate the problems they face in the business world.[25]

Of course, pastors are not unaware of the stereotypical mold in which they are cast. In fact, they begin to believe in their own inferiority with respect to status in the working world and, in so doing, help perpetuate the problem. Jacques Ellul put his finger on the matter: "To obey a calling and then to preach, to direct a congregation, to take time for soul-searching—all this seems frivolous in a world of engineers and producers. So, these embarrassed pastors also want to become technicians. They therefore practice psychoanalysis, group dynamics, social psychology, information theory, etc."[26]

The combined effect of these five conditions is to create what I have called a "shareability gap." The distance between the life of faith lived in the community of faith and the life of work lived in the community of work can be measured by the absence of an adequate language to bridge the gap between faith and ethics in business and economic life. By "adequate language" I mean a fund of shareable ideas, concepts, and vocabularies that makes the contributions of the faith intelligible to the experience of business and vice versa. When such a language is in place, a "bridge" is built across the shareability gap, permitting us to cross back and forth in a mutually enriching dialogue.

BRIDGING THE SHAREABILITY GAP

The purpose of this book is to help Christians in business to actualize their own vocation or ministry in the context of the ethical challenges of business and economic life. In the final analysis, it is those who are on the front lines who must translate the Christian vision into ethical insight and responsible action on a day-to-day basis. They have the competence and experience to understand the world of commerce and the peculiar moral demands that go with it. They have the grace and the call to be the authors of their own witness.[27]

I do not intend to pursue this purpose by proposing "Christian business ethics." There is no such thing. Rather, there are Christian ethics that shed light on issues of business ethics and, in so doing, give expression to the faith from which they flow. Moreover, there are, of course, Christians in business whose moral vision is shaped by their faith and whose responsible ethical practice is a witness to the hope that is within them. It is, once again, these practitioners who must take the lead and assume ownership for the task. Academics and theologian-ethicists like me can help only in certain ways.

However, as Charles S. McCoy has noted, whereas business insiders usually have a greater understanding of the ethical issues they face and a more realistic appraisal of the alternatives they can choose, outsiders, like academics and theologians, can open up new perspectives that business-people may not have had the time to discover or explore. Then the inter-change between insiders and outsiders, to use McCoy's terminology, becomes mutually enriching.[28]

Accordingly, I am seeking to fulfill the purpose of this book by exploring the resources of the Christian faith for the ethical life in the world of business and by bringing key themes into dialogue with the ethical issues of business and the literature of business ethics. In doing so, we will be expanding upon various points made in this chapter.

Regarding my earlier remarks about the dominance of philosophy in the field of business ethics, it should be noted, then, that this dialogical process is not antiphilosophy; philosophical ethics is a full-fledged partic-ipant in the dialogue, with something to teach and something to learn. At the same time, offering insights from faith-related ethics as a chal-lenge to the hegemony of an exclusivistic ethical rationalism in secular life does not mean that the ethics of faith are irrational! Also, we need to affirm the gift of human reason in the overall task before us. What I have been challenging is a rationalism couched in the myth of objectivity and neutrality.

Dialogue is an antidote to dualism. Dialogue is a way toward consen-sus building in a pluralistic setting. It respects the contributions of the traditions the participants represent and the dignity of each. As such, it has a moral significance of its own. Dialogue can lead us to the discovery of common values and concerns that make conversation possible and intelligible. As any remaining hopes for moral consensus through univer-sal reason dim, Christian involvement in ethical dialogue on matters of public and economic life becomes both more pressing as a need and more promising as a possibility.

In a published dialogue on the ethical resources for corporate leader-ship, business law specialist Elmer W. Johnson and distinguished Christian ethicist James M. Gustafson have given us a glimpse of what dialogue can lead to. In their brief exchange we can see how the insights of experience in business illumine the specifics of ethical issues in busi-ness and press Christian theology and ethics to shape its language for a relevant engagement with those particular concerns. At the same time, we can see theological reflection shedding new light on the reality of corporate life and, in Gustafson's words, providing "concepts and symbols by which we interpret ourselves, the circumstances of our actions, the larger ends or purposes of our actions, and the ordering of the importance of things in our lives and our world."[29]

In the final analysis, the dialogical process of this book is an experiment or exercise of thought. Dialogue involves real partners, not just an exchange of thought in the mind of one author. Nonetheless, I hope that the work begun here can help people of faith engage in that dialogue as a witness to their faith and an expression of their vocation. It can do this by providing some bridges over the shareability gap by which businesspeople can find crossings from faith to work and back again. As we pursue this purpose, we will keep in focus the gospel-centered character of Christian faith and ethics and the distinctive contribution that makes to the way we see reality, the way our characters are shaped, the values we seek, and the way we formulate our obligations and responsibilities.

People like Stan, whom we met at the beginning of the chapter, provide the inspiration for the task and, together with his colleagues in business, provide the mandate to affirm their vocation and give them more to work with in going about it.

However, before we move on to that task, we need to offer a brief qualification. Business ethics pertain to shopkeepers, clerks, electricians, and plumbers just as much as they involve corporate executives. With such a broad spectrum some choices need to be made. Although much in this book may apply to everyone at work, the issues come into sharpest focus for those in management working for corporations or similar organizations and for students preparing to enter such careers. I also hope that pastors who minister to people in business will concern themselves with these matters.

2

FROM BEING A NOBODY
TO BEING A SOMEBODY

In one of his recent columns, journalist and humorist Andy Rooney reflected on his experience attending the Kennedy Center Honors in Washington, D.C. Although it was a pleasant evening and the honorees were likeable and deserving, Rooney lamented that such events are another instance of how our society is enamored with the highly visible and famous. We seem to care little for the people who work off-camera to make the world function on a daily basis, such as business and professional people, scientists, writers, and composers.[1]

Rooney's concern that we fail to appreciate the contributions of ordinary, less visible people and focus our honors and admiration primarily on the conspicuous is instructive. He is really calling attention to a general pattern of misplaced values in our culture to which few of us seem to be immune, even the regular folks he affirms. Success and self-worth are tied to conspicuous achievements and the tangible rewards that go with them, even though those conspicuous achievements may not be the sort that produce celebrity. To say it differently, the outward symbols of success become so important that other values fade from view and may even be sacrificed.

In our work life we are especially prone to linking self-worth to generally accepted indicators of success. If we are doing well on the job and getting recognized for it or we have jobs that seem meaningful and important, we are thereby endowed with a sense of being "somebody." When we experience the opposite, we fear that we are "nobodies."

The nature of our occupations and the success we have in them are enormously powerful factors in our own sense of identity and well-being. I can recall a time in my own life, years ago, when it seemed that circumstances would conspire to end my career as a teacher and theologian. The sense of impending loss was overwhelming, and the experience of searching for work in a new and alien field was threatening; I felt out of touch with myself. This experience taught me how closely I had tied my self-worth to my job and my success in it. Although I learned a lesson from this experience, my reactions to subsequent setbacks along the career path tell me that I have not changed that much.

THE THREAT OF BEING A NOBODY

The widespread linkage between job success and self-worth means that, for many, failure on the job equates with failure in life. It constitutes the threat of being a nobody. The stronger the threat, the more blinded we may become to the moral compromises we make to achieve success. The failure-success pressure is a key factor in both morale and morality. Indeed, when moral principles are compromised for the sake of success and a sense of self-worth, we have stumbled into the irony of sacrificing personal integrity so that we can feel good about ourselves!

Robert Jackall's analysis of corporate life conveys some of this irony. He begins with the observation, "Striving for success is, of course, a moral imperative in American society."[2] Success has different purposes for different people. Some want money, others power or freedom from the control of superiors, and still others recognition and accolades.[3] For a large number of people, success is doubtless some combination of these rewards. The irony resides in the fact that, while it is a "moral imperative" to seek them, the bulk of Jackall's research suggests that success in achieving these rewards often requires setting aside other imperatives we commonly accept as moral barometers.

As Jackall acknowledges, within the corporate world there does seem to be some moral order to the quest for success: If you work hard and well, you will be rewarded with promotions and all that goes with them. In Jackall's view, however, this rule seems to work only up to a point, after which other factors become more significant, factors that provide a decidedly different ethical milieu. His research suggests that, at a certain rung on the ladder, going higher may have much more to do with social adroitness, loyalty to the ethos and structure of the corporation, and political alignments within the company.[4]

Even on the way up, hard work is not all it takes. There are other keys to success. To be appropriately dressed and groomed, to be able to hide one's emotions and respond dispassionately even to criticism directed against oneself, to use discretion in any sexual escapades, to be a team player, and to work conspicuously long hours are all factors in "making it." Then again, Jackall reports, having striking characteristics of any kind—even brilliance—is clearly detrimental, and holding views other than the ideology that is currently dominant in the corporation can be fatal. Finally, in addition to cultivating finesse and savoir-faire, one must have a "patron," a high-placed senior executive who will help the neophyte up the ladder.[5] Then the aspiring executive had better hope that that individual remains influential at the highest levels. In the end, after one has worked hard and paid attention to these keys to success, the contingency and capriciousness of organizational life, with its shake-ups and takeovers, mean that luck ends up being as big a factor as anything in realizing ambitions.[6]

Perhaps the most distressing of the success keys cited by Jackall's interviewees is the felt need to serve the current ideology, whatever it may be. One person described this as "bowing to whichever god currently holds sway."[7] This is one colorful way to voice the general observation that "bureaucracies allow their employees a diverse range of private motives for action in return for assent to common rules and official versions of reality."[8] Apart from the fact that the divorce between inward values and outward commitments is central to the problem addressed throughout this entire book, we have here yet another irony that is a cousin to the one mentioned previously. To sell out ideologically is to sacrifice the one thing needed for meaningful work and meaning in work, namely, a larger framework of meaning or a more fundamental belief system within which to place our understanding of work and by which to govern our participation in it. The work itself and success in work are not sufficient to make work meaningful; more is needed.

Joanne B. Ciulla cautions against the widely held belief that job success brings meaning and happiness to life and the companion idea that business is therefore obligated to provide so-called meaningful work. Young people fanatically pursue careers as if a good job were the sole key to happiness—whether that happiness is derived from the status of the job itself or from the wages they believe will buy it. They are willing to take drug tests, wear the right clothes, and belong to the right clubs, all in the name of obtaining a position that will eventually give them freedom to choose. Many argue that they will work a seventy-hour week, make their fortune, and retire at forty, but few ever do. This attitude has taken a social toll in terms of loneliness, divorce, child abuse, and white collar crime.[9] Ciulla points out that the more we invest in work as a source of status, meaning, and happiness, the more we expect of our jobs and the more employers attempt to meet these expectations. However, because corporations do not "possess a clear moral vision of what is good for people" and because there is no consensus as to what "meaningful work" is, all involved are headed for disappointment.[10]

Ciulla concludes that institutions can provide only general frameworks of meaning and give individuals the freedom to find meaning for themselves. Corporations do have a moral obligation to redesign jobs to make them more satisfying wherever possible. Above all, companies have an obligation to make sure that work does not stand in the way of a meaningful life outside the job. "Morality requires that corporations first recognize that employees have a right to a meaningful life. One task of business ethics is to help corporations rethink policies and practices that interfere with this right."[11]

Perhaps one of the foremost candidates for rethinking in corporate life is the kind of organizational mentality Jackall describes, in which the demand for loyalty to the currently dominant ideology creates a constant temptation to suppress one's own fundamental beliefs. To the extent that Jackall's analysis is true, at least in some places, there is a need for reform that allows for freedom of conscience and the opportunity for dialogue among people of divergent and sincere beliefs. Indeed, the effort of this study to find bridges over the "shareability gap" is in the service of this goal. If, as Ciulla contends, the first ethical obligation corporations have is to protect their employees' right to a meaningful life, then freedom of conscience and opportunity for dialogue in addressing issues of values are profound and specific instances of that moral requirement. It is a profound matter because it raises the question of the need to recognize the integrity of each individual as a responsible moral agent, which is at the core of our makeup as persons. In considering freedom of conscience and opportunity for dialogue in the workplace, we are also brought back to the particular point we are currently discussing.

From Andy Rooney's column to Joanne Ciulla's conclusions, we have observed the tendency of our culture to reward conspicuous achievement, whether it is the achievement of celebrity or the climb up the corporate ladder. As a consequence, we develop the further tendency to equate self-worth and meaningful life with conspicuous success. Erich Fromm once observed, "Since modern man experiences himself both as the seller and as the commodity to be sold on the market, his self-esteem depends on conditions beyond his control. If he is successful, he is valuable; if he is not, he is worthless."[12]

We fear being a nobody and want to be a somebody. But if being somebody means success in business, we are playing the game with a very fickle partner who can easily seduce us into compromising the very values that *do* make us somebody. Despite the importance with which we endow our occupations in determining self-worth, it is the larger framework of meaning and value to which people hold, their "faith," that gives meaning to work and the institutions of work, not the reverse. This seems to be the haunting truth behind the experience of some of Jackall's corporate citizens who must change values almost as often as they change fashions in order to keep up with their own ambitions. It is, furthermore, a logical extension of Ciulla's analysis and suggests that we need to provide workplace environments in which there is freedom of conscience and opportunity for dialogue on issues of value, where people can share the insights of their "larger frameworks of meaning." Such an approach recognizes, as Ciulla has, that corporations do not have a clear moral vision of what is good for people. That is rooted in other ground.

One executive vice president with whom I talked, a veteran of many years of the highest-level management in military and civilian life, spoke of how Scripture affirmed his life and work and, most important, provided him with the guidance he needed to keep all life's aspects in appropriate balance. Another manager in a high-pressure position with a well-known multinational spoke of how his strong sense of identity as a child of God helped him overcome the dichotomies between faith and life and integrate work life with spiritual life. His identity was in belonging to God, not in his business success.

TO BE SOMEBODY: THE UNIVERSAL PRIESTHOOD

For Christians, finding meaning and value for work and the institutions of work has often been mediated by some form of a doctrine of "vocation." Foundational to any theological elaboration of vocation and work is the idea of the universal priesthood of all believers. A key text for this is 1 Peter 2:9-10:

> But you are a chosen race, a royal priesthood, a holy nation, God's own people, in order that you may proclaim the mighty acts of him who called you out of darkness into his marvelous light.
> > Once you were not a people,
> > but now you are God's people;
> > once you had not received mercy,
> > but now you have received mercy.

Among other things, the text simply says that all God's people are called to be members of a royal priesthood or, as the Reformation teaching came to call it, the universal priesthood of all believers. To shift the focus of self-understanding from businessperson to "royal priest," without even leaving the office, is a tall order. However, that is what Peter invites us to do. Let's take a longer look at the Bible passage and reflect on some of the issues in the first part of this chapter.

Peter says that we were once not a people at all and that we lived in darkness. The imagery suggests that, from the biblical vantage point, even the most conspicuous successes among Peter's original hearers and among us now still rank as nobodies. Historically, in the biblical context, to be "not a people" means to be among the scattered gentile communities and nations and, therefore, outside the chosen, covenant people of Israel. Outside covenant relationship with God, the wealth and power of nations or of individuals were of no consequence. This theological point is underscored by the parallel idea of living in darkness. To live in darkness outside God's covenant means to live without the "marvelous light" of God's grace and that, in turn, means two things: First, it means to live without the freedom of God's forgiveness. Second, it means to live without a vision of hope.

Everyone knows about the bottom line; it has become a phrase in our daily conversation to refer to the final outcome or the most important consideration in a whole host of matters, not just profit or loss in business. The bottom line is a powerful metaphor to focus our attention on the fact that we are judged in business by results. One of Robert Jackall's sources offered the opinion that the most anxiety-provoking thing about business life is the knowledge that you are judged by the results you get, whether it is your fault or not.[13] Put negatively, there are two ways to lose: you can fail because of your own mistakes, or you can fail because of forces beyond your control in the market or in the corporation itself. Always, the threat of both is present. When self-worth is tied to the bottom line and failure is always snapping at your heels, a sense of freedom is hard to come by.

The judgment of life by results and the double jeopardy of two ways to fail can be correlated with two dimensions of a theological understanding of life under the law. Law is the name theology gives to God's word of judgment. Law has other meanings and functions than judgment, but judgment is the primary one for many theologians of the Reformation tradition and the one that concerns us for the present. That judgment, as I have said, has two dimensions.

The first dimension addresses our own failures, which result from being alienated from God. It says, in effect, "You cannot measure up." The second dimension of the law's judgment is expressed as another manifestation of our alienation from God. It is a word of judgment often voiced through the tragedies of life, which are the concrete evidence that the systems of life and the creation itself are fallen and dysfunctional. I do not mean that God brings death and suffering upon us as punishment for sin. Rather, sin, as estrangement from God, has a destructive impact on all things, and the manifestations of that destructive impact are a judgment on our alienation.

As Jackall's witness points out, we can fail because we make mistakes, but we can also fail because we are mired in a system that is imperfect and dysfunctional. Both dimensions of the law's judgment are captured in one phrase from one of the confessional liturgies of the church: "We are in bondage to sin and cannot free ourselves."[14] Sin, death, and decay are the boundaries of success for the best of us and the outer limits of hope for all of us.

But, for the God of the Bible, judgment is not the last word. In Christ Jesus there are forgiveness and new life. This is life in the Gospel as contrasted to life under law. The god of the bottom line is unforgiving. In the word of forgiveness and new life there is freedom from judgment, the freedom of knowing that we are accepted by God unconditionally. With the god of the bottom line, we are never better than a step ahead of the judgment, and our value as people is as transient as most of the friends we have when we are successful.

With the word of forgiveness and new life comes a word of hope and promise, the promise of the resurrection victory for the future of the world in the fullness of God's dominion. Even those who "make their numbers" and succeed in the tangible ways we mark success are not necessarily hopeful people. The insidious thing about staking our lives and happiness on achieving our goals is that we can always see beyond the point to which we have come. The things we attain do not themselves provide lasting satisfaction. Our vision as human beings transcends the limits of our situation at any given time. When we have reached our goals, we start looking for new goals. When we encounter poverty and war, we envision wealth and peace for all. When we see progress in realizing our dreams, we seek more progress and new dreams, for things can always be improved. Finally, we reach the point where we must ask if there is a future beyond death, a future beyond the endless repetition of past disappointments and unrealized dreams; a future for the fullness of humanity, our own and that of the entire human race. We are a future-oriented people who need a future in which to hope. That is precisely what we are given in the promise of God's future reign, the promise of everlasting life in the fullness of a creation made whole.[15]

To be called out of darkness into this marvelous light of the gospel promise is the primary sense of vocation in the Bible. *Vocation* means calling; in this case, *calling* also means conferring, for in calling us to be God's people, a royal priesthood, God confers upon us a new life: By the sheer grace of a loving God we are called from being nobody to being somebody. We are a people of freedom and hope.

This is certainly a different sense of vocation than our customary use of the word as a synonym for occupation or career. Yet this thoroughly theological and seemingly spiritual, up-in-the-clouds view of vocation provides the larger framework of meaning for understanding our occupation or career and its purpose in life. Our theological understanding of vocation reorients the way we think about work.

Nelvin Vos, a professor who thinks about these matters a great deal, expresses the new orientation to work that a Christian understanding of vocation can bring, in an article cleverly titled "To Take Life Leisurely." Vos points out that the Bible nowhere refers to work as the primary purpose of life or the basis for future rewards. Work is both good and necessary. But work is not the primary basis for human identity and worth. To give it precedence over all other aspects of our life, as the work ethic does, is to make work an idol. To worship work, to say that hard work is really the only important way to please God, is to distort the purpose for living.[16]

For Vos, a healthy view of work from the standpoint of the Christian vocation is to see it lived out with all of life in the spirit of leisure, that is, in the spirit of freedom, freedom from the compulsive drives that come with bondage to the law of results. "To live leisurely in an age of anxiety is not only to be a witness to the gift of grace from Jesus Christ, but also to serve others."[17]

The note of witness and service brings us back to our text from 1 Peter. The universal priesthood is called to proclaim the gospel of God's love in Christ, and it does so through both service and witness.

VOCATION AND OCCUPATION: FROM SELF TO SERVICE

The distinguished biblical scholar Paul S. Minear has pulled together a number of biblical threads into two salient observations about the biblical outlook on work or occupation. First of all, our occupations in life have meaning and significance in that we who pursue them are members of the community of God's people who corporately have a vocation, a calling to fulfill God's mission in the world.[18] Second, in this called community of purpose, all workers and all tasks are equally valued because all contribute to the mission and all share in the total expression of the community effort.

Equality was thus posited not on the basis of an immediate appeal to inherited rights or social utility but by reference to the horizons of God's call and by reference to the total mission of God's people. Where king and goatherd shared the same vocation, no ultimate distinction could be drawn between separate professions. Only by resisting God's intention could the adoption of special careers become the basis for invidious distinctions, self-assertive ambitions, and priorities in preferment.[19]

These features of biblical thought help to complete the contrast we have been developing between prevailing cultural norms of vocation and success and a vision of life and work from the Christian perspective. The performance-oriented outlook on success in the world of business operates with rewards and punishments that are clear and severe, and distinctions between those who have made it and those who have not are readily apparent. This is the kind of do-or-die condition of life under the law where failure can come at one's own hand or at the hand of others. However, life looked at in the light of the gospel of God's grace and forgiveness in Christ is life whose worth is given and assured by that grace, rather than by successful accomplishments.

The gospel orientation to life begets a radically different vision of the meaning of work than we normally encounter. Work has meaning in mission. Occupation has meaning in vocation. The labor of the individual has meaning in the work of the community. This is the larger framework of meaning within which to place our occupational lives. Moreover, in the gathering of former nobodies, everybody is somebody. As the quote from Paul Minear suggests, the focus is not on the conspicuous achievements of a few but on the equal dignity and importance of everyone's work as a contribution to the efforts of the whole community.

This understanding of the people of God as a people of vocation, a universal priesthood, is echoed in the companion notion of the "communion of saints," through which the Reformation transformed the idea of sainthood that prevailed in the medieval church. In that tradition and its antecedents, saints were the heroes and heroines of the faith whose lives and deeds were ones of conspicuous achievement that placed them above the general throng of Christians and commanded veneration. For Luther and other Reformation thinkers, such elevation of a few spiritual standouts was a contradiction to the central truth of the gospel that we are saved by grace through faith and not by our works. We have no righteousness to call our own but are made righteous nonetheless by the saving work of Christ. Therefore, sainthood belongs to *all* members of the household of faith, which is appropriately called the "communion of saints." Although we are grateful for the talents and dedication of those who lead in the faith, they are neither venerated nor counted more worthy of God's love.

The picture of occupation from inside vocation that we have been developing in this theological interlude is an expression of life in the gospel as contrasted with life under the law. To understand life in the gospel and occupation from inside vocation is essential to a Christian approach to business ethics. Yet, it may seem too ethereal to square with the realities of life in which janitors and managers are, in fact, paid different salaries and enjoy vastly different social and economic privileges commensurate with their relative achievements. In such a context, it is hard to see evidence of any community, including the churches, in which the biblical ideal is really at work, and it is hard to believe in it under the circumstances of the here and now. Certainly, even the most devoted Christians, remaining, as they do, sinners while yet being saints, are readily tempted into leading their lives under the rule of the modern success ethos, forgetting the gospel for the seductive allure of the law.

Author Suzanne Gordon includes some examples of recent feminist self-criticism in her analysis of how women have been faring in business. One striking case history is provided by Mary Anne Dolan, who told of becoming editor of the *Miami Herald* and, with great expectations, hiring women into positions of power and authority. The dream was of a workplace where "feminine" qualities of nurture, warmth, respect, and generosity would supplant the hard-driving characteristics of traditional individualism and competitiveness. Instead, "the power grab began.... In the unique laboratory of the *Herald,* women given large doses of power were transmogrified by it. Faced with the freedom to behave differently from the iconic male executive, the women chose the course of least change."[20]

Gordon goes on, in the next chapter of her book, to document how the resurgent commitment in our society to the ideal of personal success in business or professional life has driven both men and women into exceedingly long work hours and a preoccupation with work to the degree that virtually all other values of life are crowded out.[21] We will return to Gordon's analysis at a later point. For now it is sufficient to point out that Dolan's account and Gordon's own research serve to punctuate our observations that commitment to a "religion" of conspicuous achievement as the key to meaning in life can be a harsh and demanding regimen that could cause us to compromise our own best qualities and some of our most precious values.

To view occupation and self-worth from inside gospel vocation as we have been doing may indeed seem to be an elusive, other-worldly ideal, but if it is absent from our down-to-earth understanding and outlook on life and work, we could lose our souls. In fact, this spiritual ideal has practical implications for the ethics of business: It reorients our values by shifting our focus from concern for self to service to others.

FROM SELF TO SERVICE:
AMBITION TRANSVALUED

Martin Luther's famous treatise *On Christian Liberty,* begins with the
seemingly contradictory statement that the Christian is perfectly free and
subject to no one and, at the same time, a dutiful servant to all people.
The freedom spoken of here is freedom from the condemnation of the
law. This freedom is ours through the forgiveness of sins we have in
Christ. Being thereby accepted by God unconditionally, we are free
from worry about ourselves, free from fear of the law and meeting its
demands, and free for service to others. By the grace of God, we are
moved from self to service, service that is uncoerced by fear or ambition
and service that is freely given by those who are already secure in their
self-worth as forgiven children of God. We love as we have first been
loved. We are, as Luther put it, "Christs" to each other and, by making
Christ present in our own loving service, we fulfill the vocation of
priesthood.[22]

It is not surprising, then, that Luther's emphasis in discussing the purpose of our various occupations in life would be one of service. For
Luther, vocation is realized through the various "stations" we occupy in
life: parenting, citizenship, marriage, work, profession, and so on. These
are roles and relationships that God has established to benefit all people,
and all who participate in them participate in that plan. For Christians in
particular, the stations of life are conduits for the loving service of people
free in the gospel.[23] In and through the daily "vocations" or occupations
of life, we have an avenue for the expression of our priestly vocation
even as we participate in God's general providential plan. In chapter 4
we will return to Luther's doctrine of vocation and look at the light it
sheds on the nature and purpose of business as an institution. For now it
is important to note that, first of all, Luther's orientation to work for the
individual Christian springs from the freedom of life in the gospel.
Second, the services rendered through work and the other occupations
of life, by Christians and others, are part of God's plan for the common
good.

By seeing the stations of life as channels of God's love and providential care for humanity, Luther was able to give new vocational meaning
to work, professional life, government, and family life as integral to
God's plan and purposes for the world. At last, all people were endowed
with a sense of calling from God, not only those who had embraced the
monastic ideal or entered the ranks of the clergy.

Calvin followed Luther in conferring religious dignity and theological
significance on daily work. This is evident in his commentary on the

story of Mary and Martha (Luke 10:38-42). In the medieval tradition, this story was interpreted as evidence that Jesus commended the contemplative life by affirming Mary for her attentiveness to his teaching and rebuking Martha for being too busy with dinner preparations to sit at his feet. Calvin overturned this interpretation by pointing out that Jesus' comments were restricted to the specific characteristics of that incident and not in any way a general denigration of labor and the service of work.[24] Calvin concludes that "we know that men were created for the express purpose of being employed in labour of various kinds, and that no sacrifice is more pleasing to God than when every man applies diligently to his own calling, and endeavors to live in such a manner as to contribute to the general advantage."[25]

As Lee Hardy has pointed out in his historical study, the strong Protestant tradition on vocation and the dignity of work has been appropriated by contemporary Roman Catholic thought. There are already intimations of an appreciation for the Reformation doctrine of vocation in the papal encyclical *Rerum Novarum* of 1891. With Pope John Paul II's *Laborum Exercens* in 1981, we see virtual agreement at every major point.[26]

Not only is work revalued in the movement from self to service, but the ambition we associate with the success imperative in modern business is also transvalued. Ambition for the advancement of oneself is not intrinsically evil, and certainly a business enterprise that is not in some real, material sense successful is also not able to survive and provide value and wealth for the benefit of the community. Our effort in the preceding has been to place ambition and success into a larger framework of meaning and thereby place it in a healthier perspective. Within that larger perspective of our gospel vocation, we can see the movement from self to service as a new life of freedom in which our natural ambitions and drives to succeed can be freed from the burden of being the key to self-worth and redirected to the goals of service to the needs of our neighbor.

When looked at in this light, striving to do your best in the faithful pursuit of a business vocation is a way to serve others—from the support of one's family to the support of one's community—that ranks right along with parenting, civic service, government, or work in one of the helping professions. It need not be caricatured as an exercise in self-aggrandizement.

Not long ago I had the pleasure of meeting with a Christian businessman who had founded and headed up a large business with many franchises that employed a large number of young people. Two things he told me about his career stand out. First, he consistently reinvested in the business rather than take immediate profits for himself because expanding the business expanded the opportunities for others to participate. Second, he impressed on his managers their responsibility to be role models for the large numbers of young people who worked for them. For most of the new employees, it would be their first experience in the world of work, and he wanted to be sure that it was a good one, characterized by solid ethics and humane management.

ETHICS AS WITNESS

The theme of "self to service" has been developed as a Christian perspective on work that challenges the prevailing ethos of business life as understood and described by those who live it and by those who have studied and analyzed it. No institution as multifaceted and far-flung as "business" can be adequately understood in terms of one description or version of it. Other versions of the ethos of business life come from different quarters than we have sampled. Certainly in the chapters ahead we will see trends in ethical business that seek to create a more humane atmosphere, one that respects the individual values that people bring with them to the job. Nonetheless, the success imperative remains a driving force for businesspeople in our society and, indeed, for others in other occupations, including the clergy and the denizens of the academic world! By engaging it as we have, we have begun the dialogue promised in chapter 1, I hope in a way that connects with people's experience and concerns. We will develop this dialogue further as we relate the various implications of the self-to-service theme to the issues that follow, especially those in chapters 5 and 6.

In starting the dialogue by talking about occupation from inside Christian vocation, we have also set the stage for dealing with our call to witness to the gospel promise. For the Christian community, ethics are part and parcel of its witness in the world. Our service to others in love calls attention to God's self-giving love in Jesus Christ. The values we seek, we seek because they are values God has promised to realize, in their fullness, in the fullness of God's coming reign. We have a vision of what those values are in the vision of that future dominion of God that is revealed in Jesus' resurrection victory over sin and death. To seek these goods, then, witnesses to the hope that is within us and anticipates the things God has promised.

In other words, when Christians stand for the value of all life by standing against the wanton use of abortion or by standing for the acceptance, rights, and opportunities of the disabled, they anticipate the fullness of life that is part of the gospel promise for the reign of God. When Christians become advocates for a public policy that can help provide a greater measure of health care for all people or when they become an influence for a sexual ethic that celebrates the joy of bodily life and respects it as an integral part of the self, they are acting in anticipation of the value of wholeness that is part of the promise of the reign of God. When Christians become active agents of reconciliation at every level of life, from nuclear family to international family, they anticipate the promise of peace that is a part of their hope for the dominion of God. When Christians oppose racism, sexism, and other isms that exclude and denigrate people for being what they are, they anticipate the value of equality that is part of our hope for the future reign of God.[27]

If vocation involves witness, and ethics are part of witness, we are back to the issues raised in chapter 1 of how we bridge the shareability gap and carry forward our vocation in the world of work. A recent cartoon in *Commonweal* shows a number of businesspeople sitting around the boardroom table. One man, seated at the end, is looking sheepish as the chairman yells at him: "We appreciate your quotations from Plato, Simpkins, however, they do not apply to this little takeover!"[28] The cartoon reminds us once more that bridging the gap will not be easy. For many in business, the above theological discussion and the witness we want to make in and through business ethics will seem as out of place as Simpkins's quotations of Plato. However, difficulty does not equal futility, and we are not without encouragement.

In Matthew 13:1-9 we read the familiar parable of the sower. The parable tells us that some seed did not grow to maturity and produce grain because it fell on the path and was eaten by birds, had shallow roots in rocky soil, or was choked by thorns. That same chapter later explains how the seeds that fell on the path, on rocky soil, or among thorns represent people who for various reasons do not believe or do not hold fast to the gospel promise of God's coming reign. This is the explanation we most often hear discussed, frequently in moralistic terms, warning us, for example, not to be like the seed that fell among thorns, where the word was choked by "the cares of the world and the lure of wealth" (13:22).

The real punch line of the parable, however, appears to be the verse that tells us that there was seed that fell on good soil and produced abundantly. To the disciples, who were probably discouraged at times that their mission was making little progress, this parable reassured them that God's reign would come and that there was, despite all obstacles, no stopping it.

3

THE NOT-SO-SECULAR WORLD

The fall of communism can be regarded as a sign that modern thought—based on the premise that the world is objectively knowable, and that the knowledge so obtained can be absolutely generalized—has come to a final crisis. This era has created the first global, or planetary, technical civilization, but it has reached the limit of its potential, the point beyond which the abyss begins. I think the end of communism is a serious warning to all mankind. It is a signal that the era of arrogant, absolutive reason is drawing to a close and it is high time to draw conclusions from that fact.[1]

—VACLAV HAVEL

One of the ways in which the shareability gap is perpetuated is the continued belief that secularity is the final truth about reality. That belief is implicit in several of the five conditions discussed in the opening chapter, but it is most apparent in the one referring to our lingering conviction that there is a genuinely "universal reason" that can provide generally accepted answers to our problems of ethics.

Two decades ago, at one of the more recent peak periods of secular consciousness in our society, one theologian noted six signs of secularization: (1) religious institutions, symbols, and doctrines have lost much of their influence; (2) religious institutions have become sufficiently secular that their members are hard to distinguish from those who do not practice religion; (3) the autonomy of the public sector has been almost completely secured from religious interference; (4) history has no divinely ordained goal, and humanity is the measure of all that is happening in the world; (5) the natural world has been desacralized and given over to technology; and (6) loss of religion leads to a loss of moral authority.[2] In a secular worldview, religion, custom, cultural tradition, and other expressions of the human spirit must bow to detached, objective reason and empirical knowledge and take up permanent residence in the personal and private realm of subjectivity.

Secularization has continued unabated but not without reevaluation. As we have already seen, people are increasingly aware of the limits of

28

rational and empirical thought to give, on its own, an adequate account of human experience. We have entered what many observers consider to be a postmodern or post-Enlightenment era in which confidence in our ability to achieve uniformity of thought and greater control of life through pure reason by dealing with hard facts is being replaced by a growing appreciation for the importance of religion, ethnicity, gender, cultural relativity, and socioeconomic location as the ineluctable forces shaping our perceptions of reality in our pluralistic world.

If secularization was a humanistic emancipation of the world from the tyranny of religious authoritarianism and superstitious conventions, the emerging affirmation of our pluralism in this postmodern era could well be a new humanistic emancipation from the distortion of secularism—an almost "religious," ideological form of secularization that advocates detached reason and empirical research to the exclusion of all other ways of knowing. This is the thrust of the statement by Vaclav Havel, president of the Czech Republic, delivered in a speech at the World Economic Forum in Davos, Switzerland, on February 4, 1992. In his stirring remarks he singles out communism, but communism is but one particularly virulent form of "arrogant, absolutive" reason, which begins as a triumph of humanism and ends as the prison of the human spirit. Thus, Havel observes eloquently: "Communism was not defeated by military force, but by life, by the human spirit, by conscience, by the resistance of Being and man to manipulation. It was defeated by a revolt of color, authenticity, history in all its variety, and human individuality against imprisonment within a uniform ideology."[3]

Havel goes on to say that this radical change in the world situation is disconcerting and confusing. Not only must we face the loss of some of the modern era's most cherished ways of looking at the world but also we must face the fact that they have not served us well. That conclusion seems inescapable when we survey the wreckage of modernity: the environmental crisis, the growing gulf between the rich and the poor, the spread of AIDS, and the threat of regional wars. Says Havel, "Modern man, proud of having used impersonal reason to release a giant genie from its bottle, is now impersonally distressed to find he can't drive it back into the bottle again."[4] We cannot do it because we are trying to employ the same means that got us into trouble to get us out: a new ideology, a new technology, and so on. "We are looking for an objective way out of the crisis of objectivism. Everything would seem to suggest that this is not the way to go."[5]

In Heinrich Böll's antiwar, antitotalitarian novel, *Billiards at Half-Past Nine*, Robert Faehmel, the protagonist, tells how, although an architect by training, he has never built the homes and churches he dreamed of building. He has only blown them up. The German army, knowing his knowledge of architecture, turned him into a demolitions expert during World War II. He blew up homes and churches in that capacity because his lunatic general kept wanting a "field of fire," the removal of all obstacles, such as buildings, to firing directly at the oncoming enemy. The idea of creating a field of fire was insane because it was obsolete in the era of air power. Nonetheless, Faehmel followed orders until, finally, three days before the end of the war he blew up St. Anthony's Abbey to give the retreating German army a field of fire it did not need. St. Anthony's was his father's crowning achievement as an architect.

In this parable is captured some of the irony of Havel's warning that the way out cannot be the same as the way in. Obsolete techniques, when perpetuated beyond their usefulness, become ideological habits that can destroy or stifle some of the most precious expressions of the human spirit. Havel's conclusion seems fitting, then: "In a world global civilization, only those who are looking for a technical trick to save civilization need feel despair. But those who believe, in all modesty, in the mysterious power of their own human Being, which mediates between them and the mysterious power of the world's Being, have no reason to despair at all."[6]

In the end, Havel's realism is capped by a note of hope that echoes, in its own way, the bottom-line message of the parable of the Sower. It suggests the new opportunity for the witness of the religious spirit in our world, a suggestion that fits the orientation of this book. At the same time, Havel's warning against any renewal of absolutist claims for reason can be issued to religion as well. The new situation demands something different from everyone in this not-so-secular world. It is with the blend of realism, caution, and hope that Havel provides that we move forward to explore this new situation, especially as it applies to ethics in business.

OUR MODERN HERITAGE OF ETHICAL UNCERTAINTY

The Enlightenment project to build a moral and just world order on the foundations of reason has failed. This conclusion is argued convincingly by Alasdair MacIntyre, a Notre Dame philosopher whose 1981 book, *After Virtue,* has become one of the most influential analyses of the current state of ethics in our society. Our first clue to the truth of this thesis is the nature of contemporary moral debates; they never end! Rivals in the debates both mount carefully reasoned arguments for their positions, but rational argumentation is not capable of decisively resolving the issue in favor of one side or the other.[7]

The failure of reason to settle its own ethical disputes leaves the door open to emotivism. Emotivism operates with the premise that all moral judgments are essentially expressions of emotion, of attitudes or feelings, both positive and negative, about certain behaviors and values. To say something is good is, in effect, to say "I approve" or "Hurray for that!" It is a highly personal and subjective judgment, even though it may be shared by many others. Reason cannot resolve moral disputes because they are not matters amenable to rational criteria; they are matters of feeling. Reason deals with matters of fact for which there are appropriate rational criteria, such as empirical tests, for determining the truth and falsity of statements.[8]

The emotivist viewpoint is obviously a highly relativistic, individualistic approach to ethics in which there are really no objective moral claims one can insist all should honor. A popular version of this theory surfaced in the 1960s counterculture phrase, "If it feels good, do it!" However, MacIntyre is not simply saying that emotivism, in its serious philosophical mode as well as its simplistic popular expressions, is just one theory of morality contending for acceptance alongside others. He asserts that emotivism is embodied in the culture and that we, in fact, operate as if emotivism were true.

MacIntyre offers one example of how emotivism imbues our culture that is particularly pertinent to business ethics concerns. He describes how certain social types or characters come to typify a given society and shape its culture and ethos by being emblematic of its underlying convictions. In our emotivist society one of the key types that define the culture and shape its ethic is the bureaucratic manager, whether in business, government, or some other institution.[9]

It is characteristic of the manager that he or she is judged by effectiveness in matching means and ends for the most favorable cost-benefit ratio or bottom line. Effectiveness, in the end, is simply "successful power," which is the justification for the manager's authority and the benefits that accrue to success. Such a limited, almost amoral basis for authority could exist only in an emotivist culture. The authority of the manager is in no wise grounded in certain objective values produced or subject to evaluation in the light of generally accepted, rationally argued norms. After all, the basic premise of emotivism is that reason cannot establish objective values or universal norms. All faiths, moral theories, or expressions of conscience are equally nonrational. With no norms or values incumbent upon managers, they are "free" to choose that outlook that best serves the effectiveness of the organization and set about the task of coaxing or coercing conformity and suppressing conflict among subordinates.[10]

As MacIntyre's thesis unfolds, several connections with ideas we have been working on begin to appear. James Kuhn and Donald Shriver have observed that bureaucratic life and management à la MacIntyre bear a close family resemblance to the portrait Jackall paints. However, the likeness is more than an interesting comparison. Kuhn and Shriver see in MacIntyre's analysis the roots of Jackall's discovery that personal values and convictions must be suppressed on the job and one's private life ethics segregated from one's business life ethics. Such a separation not only is threatening to the integrity or wholeness of the individual but can end up impoverishing the organization as well.[11]

In America do we not expect people to observe a certain decent separation between their personal values and the specialized work they perform on the job or in a profession? Young people pledging limited, self-interested loyalty to their corporate jobs, as many appear to be doing in recent years, make clear their acceptance of such a separation. A job supports their ability to put into practice the other values of their lives in settings as diverse as family, church, vocation, and friendship. But the price of this segregation of values in one's life can be high for the person, and separation of employees' personal lives from organizational life can exact a high cost for the corporation itself.

With these observations we add some depth and texture to our understanding of the dualism between personal morality and business ethics identified in chapter 1 as an integral part of the problem we seek to address. Moreover, in the light of MacIntyre's analysis, the lingering trust in objective reason as the basis for a common morality and the corollary dominance of moral philosophy and empirical research in the field of business ethics—points also brought out in chapter 1—constitute more than a frustration to the witness of faith in business ethics. These phenomena are a potential source of self-deception for business because, if we live as though emotivism were true and all consciences were equal, then business with the help of the academy is trying to build the edifice of ethics on a rational-empirical foundation that has lost its authority in our society! Such self-deception, when recognized openly or tacitly, easily breeds a moral cynicism that permeates the whole organization.

Systemic moral cynicism is a hostile environment for the nurture and growth of individual ethical integrity, not only by providing little incentive for integrity but also by punishing its expression through direct or indirect means. A pertinent example is that of whistle-blowers, who feel compelled to bring what they believe is unethical behavior in their organization to the attention of management, government agencies, or the public media. To be sure, not all who blow the whistle on their company or the people working in it do so out of high moral principle; some seek revenge or personal gain. However, many proceed with integrity and have most often been rewarded for their courage and veracity by being subjected to discrimination and even loss of job.

Respect for truth and authentic commitment to high ethical standards, combined with just processes for evaluating and acting upon the claims of the whistle-blower—even company policies that encourage whistle-blowing—need to be integral parts of the corporate system and culture of an organization. All the ethical codes and commitments an organization may affirm will not encourage or reward truthfulness if the ethical standards espoused have no authority in the real life and operative beliefs of the corporate community, that is, if moral cynicism is a pervasive undercurrent.[12]

To the extent that individual integrity is frustrated, the organization is weakened and, in fact, may lose more than just the loyalty and contribution of the individual; talented people of high principle often simply leave. I had the pleasure of spending the afternoon with the president of a small but highly successful marketing and communications firm who did just that. We can call him George. George started his own business so that he could have the freedom to follow his own conscience, reject morally questionable contracts, and build an organization marked by people who are trustworthy and morally sensitive.

In addition, George pointed out that other values he prized, such as being client-centered, are often hard to sustain in many large corporations, where services to the client can be superseded by service to the ambitions of superiors. In general, good relationships were high on his business ethics agenda. He wanted to foster the kinds of relationships that instill confidence and trust among employees and with clients and other businesses. In an atmosphere of moral cynicism, where greed favors short-term profit over long-term values, relational commitments get left in the dust.

George gave a deceptively simple example of a practice that shows concern for others and builds trust and confidence; he pays his bills on time. He sees this as a significant ethical obligation because others need that money for their daily business just as he needs a dependable cash flow for his operation. This particular example is memorable because it contrasts starkly with the situation described to me by a young middle manager in a large plastics manufacturing company. This firm is riding the crest of opportunities for rapid growth. However, one of the ways they are taking advantage of growth opportunities is to use much of their cash flow to leverage new initiatives. As a result, bills are not paid on time. "They're doing business with other people's money," my young middle manager complained. "When suppliers get fed up, management simply looks for a new supplier. So far they've been getting away with it." How will this manager cope with his qualms of conscience about the practices of his superiors? He feels he is too far down the ladder to effect change, and he is doubtless right. He does not have George's wherewithal to start his own business. If he gets a chance at a good job with another company, he will probably leave but, in the meantime, as a Christian he struggles; if he leaves, moreover, he leaves the situation untouched by his witness. The plight of ethically sensitive people who lack the clout to create change unveils another face of moral cynicism: in the absence of overriding moral authority expressed through structures of organizational governance, power finally decides what the operative morality (or lack of it) will be. This brings us back to the main lines of our current discussion.

For MacIntyre the failure of Enlightenment rationalism to establish a moral consensus is rooted in its secularist rejection of any ideal of human fulfillment. Catholic and Protestant theology, as well as Greek humanism, had provided Western culture with an understanding of humanity's true end, a vision of what authentic human life is all about. However, secularism rejected all of these visions. The purpose of morality, MacIntyre points out, is to bring people to the realization of true fulfillment in the human ideal. Therefore, ethical principles in the classical and Christian traditions were forged with their respective visions of the end of humanity in mind. Because there is no longer an authoritative vision of such an end, the ethical precepts it spawned are empty of meaning and authority, even though we continue to invoke them.[13]

ETHICS IN A PLURALISTIC WORLD

To live in a society in which people operate as though emotivism were true and live without the benefit of a unifying vision of true humanity is to live in a pluralistic world of diverse moral convictions and diverse versions of the human good based on a diversity of cultural and religious traditions and differences in social and economic location.

Ronald Thiemann, dean of Harvard Divinity School, talks of this pluralistic world as a place of "ethical vertigo." Without an authoritative moral tradition or comprehensive religious vision, it is like a world without a horizon. "A world without a horizon is a world without balance."[14] In words that echo MacIntyre, he says:

> This new pluralism will be sustained by the conviction that opposing positions regarding abortion or nuclear disarmament or social welfare programs are simply equally unjustifiable opinions that express the personal preferences of those who hold them. There are no reasons or arguments that can ultimately decide such matters, and thus they must be simply decided by the exercise of power (a position clearly illustrated by the recent tragic bombings of abortion clinics).[15]

The impact of pluralism on ethics, particularly at the level of public policy, is abundantly clear when we view some of the hot issues in the realm of biomedical ethics. One of the more controversial is the question of whether individuals should have the right to voluntary euthanasia or assisted suicide. H. Tristram Englehart Jr., a professor of medicine and a highly respected contributor to the literature of medical ethics, has questioned whether it is possible for the state to demonstrate adequate grounds for the prohibition of voluntary euthanasia and assisted suicide. In his mind it is doubtful. The state can no longer claim a normative view of the moral life by which to justify policies of prohibition, let alone rest its authority in a secular world on an appeal to divine sanctions. Restrictions on the practice might be placed on those who are not terminally ill in view of obligations to others, such as a spouse or the military. However, that is about as far as we are likely to be able to go in the future regulation of voluntary euthanasia or assisted suicide. "One is likely to get much less from general secular ethics than one had originally hoped.... In a secular, pluralist society one will need to accept euthanasia by default."[16]

When we return our gaze to the particularities of business ethics in a pluralistic context, the issue of pluralism is immediately expanded. Thus far, we have tacitly been dealing with ethical diversity and the loss of moral consensus largely in terms of developments in the secularization of the Western world.

With the rapid globalization of business, issues of international business ethics are fast becoming some of the most urgent matters on the general business ethics agenda. This being the case, the challenge of pluralism to ethics is intensified and complicated by stirring the ingredients of international diversity into the mix. Businesspeople selling insurance in western Texas or making widgets for consumers in the southeastern United States may be tempted to put this one on the back burner as beyond their normal experience and concern. However, this is increasingly hard to do as international commerce becomes more a part of the fabric of our society and the integrity of our national industries in international dealings becomes a concern for all of us.

Thomas Donaldson, professor of business ethics at Georgetown University, has written a book on international business ethics in which he raises the question that is invariably raised by the reality of ethical pluralism: Does the fact that we can observe a certain cultural relativity in ethical standards worldwide mean that we are consigned to total relativity in ethics? If ethical relativism is true, there are, in fact, no ethical principles or traditions that can be preferred, and in that moral vacuum issues will doubtless be decided by economic power and expediency.[17] Thus, shall we market hazardous pesticides in poor countries that cannot afford to protect life by enforcing the same safety standards that obtain in affluent countries? In the absence of any generally accepted moral constraints, there is no reason to let anything but the bottom line decide.

Donaldson believes that there is a way out of ethical relativism and commends for us a version of the social contract theory that spells out the duties and limitation of duties that multinational companies have in relation to the rights of people in other countries where they operate.[18] The details of his version of social contract theory and of the specific duties he sets forth need not detain us at this juncture. The thing to note is that Donaldson believes these duties can be determined with reference to commonly held views that humans have rights and we all know what they are. How can such an assumption be defended in a pluralistic world, notwithstanding the existence of a United Nations Declaration of Human Rights?

For the distinguished theologian Hans Küng, the possibility of universal or absolute norms of ethical obligation such as human rights resides with religion. People without religious commitments can, of course, be moral and lead exemplary lives. However, only religious foundations have the *transcendent* character that can elevate ethical commitments above the self-interest of individuals and groups. Unconditional ethical demands such as those represented by human rights—rights that embody a notion of the universal human good, recalling MacIntyre's concern—cannot be derived from the finite conditions of human existence (which includes finite secular reason, I would add).[19]

There is an irony in Küng's claim. The secularized rationalism of the Enlightenment era has done its work so well in emancipating humanity from the control of religion that, in its failure to establish a new moral consensus based on reason, it has brought religion into sharper focus as the key to the recovery of moral authority. Moreover, recalling my earlier comment to this effect, such a recovery under the auspices of religious faith would, in turn, be an emancipation of humankind from the limiting and frustrating controls of rationalism. Küng puts it this way:

> At least for the prophetic religions—Judaism, Christianity and Islam—it is the one unconditional in all that is conditioned that can provide a basis for the absoluteness and universality of ethical demands, that primal ground, primal support, primal goal of human beings and the world we call God. *This primal ground, primal support and primal goal does not represent alien control over human beings. On the contrary: such grounding, anchorage and direction open up the possibility for true human selfhood and action; they make it possible to frame rules for oneself and to accept personal responsibility.*[20]

Küng's statements bring us back to our concern for the witness of the Christian community in the world.

PLURALISM AND THE CHRISTIAN WITNESS

The December 9, 1991, *Time* cover story deals with the ongoing divisions in American society over the proper role of religion in public life. Some who feel the separation of church and state has gone too far argue for a greater accommodation of religious viewpoints in everything from religious displays, like manger scenes in public places at Christmas time, to what is included in public school textbooks. Opponents want the incursion of religious ideas to be strictly regulated. The article concludes with these remarkable words:

> For God to be kept out of the classroom or out of America's public debate by nervous school administrators or overcautious politicians serves no one's interests. That restriction prevents people from drawing on this country's rich and diverse religious heritage for guidance, *and it degrades the nation's moral discourse by placing the whole realm of theological reasoning out of bounds. The price of that sort of quarantine, at a time of moral dislocation, is—and has been—far too high.*[21]

Time's testimony from our not-so-secular world is a fitting prelude to the resumption of our primary task of understanding and pursuing the Christian witness in the business ethics of today's pluralistic world, a vital element in bridging the shareability gap.

The failure of moral consensus under secular rationalism and the pluralism that has emerged in its wake has brought a new appreciation for "particularity." *Particularity* refers to the fact that our view of reality, our values, and our moral convictions are shaped by the particular forces of religion, culture, ethnicity, and socioeconomic vocation predominant in our lives. Appreciation of particularity and the contribution each particular heritage brings as a needed part of our whole grip on the understanding of life explains in large measure the kind of new openness signaled by the conclusion of the *Time* article. It is an openness to the significant—if not essential—contribution of religion to public life. The ground seems fertile for a new consideration of religious witness in the affairs of human life, *including business life.*

At the same time, in our pluralistic world the ground is also fertile for moral cynicism and a new virulent secularism of ethical relativism. There is plenty of evidence to suggest that MacIntyre was right in 1982, when he said that we live in an emotivist society, and that he is still right.

Nonetheless, in terms of our focus on business, I have stressed the expressed desire of people in business to make the contribution their faith provides to the development of sound business ethics at a time when a renewal of confidence in the ethics of the business community is much in need. Moreover, there are signs that this contribution is being made by conscientious Christians and that these contributions have a chance in an atmosphere where more and more business leaders are showing some restiveness with what sometimes seems to be our state of moral anarchy.

In this rather ambiguous situation, Ronald Thiemann's proposal for a "public theology" provides some helpful insights. Thiemann's purposes, at least in some respects, appear not unlike our own. He wants to provide resources from Christian theology "to enable people of faith to regain a public voice in our pluralistic culture."[22] This will require a public theology that avoids the twin perils of trying to gain a hearing by too much accommodation to the language and concepts of secular culture, on the one hand, and a militant sectarian witness, on the other hand. In other words, a public theology must speak to the issues of the day by maintaining the integrity of its biblical and theological tradition but in a manner sensitive to our pluralistic world.[23]

"Public theology is faith seeking to understand the relation between Christian convictions and the broader social and cultural context within which the Christian community lives...to identify the particular places where Christian convictions intersect with the practices of contemporary political life."[24] Public theology proceeds with confidence that the insights of the faith offer valid and relevant guidance for dealing with current ethical issues. But it is the confidence of *faith,* and that is important to emphasize. There can be little confidence that, in the pluralistic, ambiguous situation we have described, religion and secular rationalism will forge a common bond and create a new synthesis of human thought and belief to restore the moral authority MacIntyre has shown is lost. Again, I quote Thiemann:

> The goal of establishing some common ground between the Christian faith and secular rational inquiry is surely a noble one, but at this moment in our history the best we can hope for is a series of temporary and ad hoc alliances between theology and the resources of our culture. Any more permanent covenant between, for example, Christian belief and rational inquiry becomes suspect in large part because rational inquiry has increasingly sought to identify itself with unbelief.[25]

Notwithstanding this important caution, Thiemann does not want to say that there can be no common human values or virtues that we can mutually affirm and appreciate. The point is to find a path between the extremes of secular or religious imperialism, on the one hand, and ethical relativism, on the other.[26] Although Thiemann's project is finally somewhat different in purpose and focus than the one we are pursuing, his important work in developing the stance of public theology in the milieu of pluralism provides, I believe, a congenial and helpful rationale for proceeding along the path of dialogue. Moreover, it is a rationale that realistically deals with the deep ambiguity of pluralism that has become apparent in our discussion, while yet blending that realism with hope for a renewed Christian witness in our time.

RATIONALISM, REASON, AND RELIGION: TRANSITIONAL COMMENTS

We have identified the desire and the need for faith to speak to ethics in business, and we have noted some of the conditions that frustrate it. We have seen that Christians are called to speak and, in that calling, to discover a lifestyle of service, which is itself a profound mode of speaking that promises guidance to the orientation and practice of ethics in business. We have charted some of the opportunities and challenges of our cultural context in a postmodern, pluralistic, not-so-secular world. We have suggested that dialogue is an appropriate way to speak and have made a modest beginning of that dialogue in our exploration of vocation. We have also hinted that such dialogue, to be effective, will need to be both a clear statement of Christian perspectives and respectful of the realities of contemporary pluralism at home and in the arena of international business. Now we need to find a model for dialogue that is appropriate as a means of witness to the Christian faith and appropriate in the context of business.

Before we go forward with this agenda, however, I think a few more words are needed on the relationship of rationalism, reason, and religion. Earlier I made the point, in effect, that our criticism of the limits and pretensions of secular rationalism does not mean that religion is the irrational alternative for the foundations of ethics. I hope that by now it is apparent that what I have most often referred to as "secular rationalism" is not simply another name for "reason" in general. Secular rationalism rather refers to that development of our modern world in which rational and empirical inquiry is thought to be capable of leading us to objective truth about all things, without any influences of an emotive or spiritual sort, including the claims of religion.

Even if this distinction has been made clear, however, it is still the case that some tend to think of religion and even morality in general as irrational. In the field of business ethics, Laura Nash casts the matter in just those terms. Following some of the ideas of the eighteenth-century philosopher David Hume and the contemporary philosopher Amitai Etzioni, Nash sees the resources of morality within the human spirit and the impulses to moral behavior they produce to be irrational: "Whether the source of such impulses is religion or culture or the preference of one's parents, the irrationality of moral reasoning and behavior is a fact. To construct a business ethic that works only on commercial logic to motivate ethical behavior is to fail to draw on that deep reservoir of spontaneous decency."[27]

I believe that labeling morality and religion in this way is unfortunate because it reinforces the dualism between the things of the spirit and the things of commerce; it potentially widens the shareability gap, and it plays into the hands of emotivism and relativity. In fairness to Laura Nash, whose work we will look at with appreciation in a later chapter, her point is to contrast the positive richness of human moral sensibilities with the narrow reasoning of the stereotypical business mind. Therefore, even if she is somewhat overoptimistic about the impulses of the human spirit, her real purpose is not outside our own. It would simply be more helpful to take a broader view of rationality, one that includes religion and morality, and contrast that with the narrower "commercial logic" followed so strictly by many in business.

In making that suggestion, of course, it is incumbent upon me to demonstrate in what sense religion and morality are rational. To do so would engage us in an extensive philosophical debate that is, in any case, unresolved. This enterprise, although relevant, is beyond our scope. However, I can at least stake out my perspective on this issue with a brief account of a broader perspective on rationality that leaves room for morality and religion within its boundaries.

Religious belief and ethical reflection share rationality with other beliefs in that they are engaged in constructing a coherent scheme by which one is able to make sense of reality and the ultimate concern for the human good and the good of the planet. In this sense, even the theologian and the scientist stand on common ground: For all the objectivity of empirical research, interpretation of the significance of its results, even the description of the results themselves, requires language and concepts that reflect a larger framework of meaning, coherent beliefs about reality that are not themselves the product of demonstrable proofs. This means, of course, that in a pluralistic world the variety of schemes that are constructed out of the diverse particularities of human experience will not only coexist and compete but also command our respect and consideration. However, it does not mean that a dialogue among them will not produce a discovery of common grounds or points of operative consensus in ethics, and it does not mean that critical evaluation by reasoned argumentation is not possible; both are inherent in the dialogical process.

In the account of Jesus' trial before Pilate as recorded in the Gospel of John, Jesus says to Pilate, "Everyone who belongs to the truth listens to my voice" (18:37). Pilate's well-known reply is, "What is truth?" (v. 38). One commentator calls this response "typical of the cynical skepticism of the Roman mind."[28] What is interesting about this observation is that cynicism about the possibility of the truth breeds moral cynicism as well, for Pilate then condemned Jesus to death even though he had already stated that there was no empirical evidence by which to convict him. In so doing, Pilate acted *irrationally*.

4

FROM DUALISM TO DIALOGUE

Trust. Honor. Loyalty. Three words that have little meaning today. Doctors check credit references before treating the ill; publishers value commercialism over literary excellence; holidays revolve around shopping and parties, not family and religion; policemen, baseball players, and teachers—once role models for children—are now accused of savagely beating citizens, betting on sporting events, and altering student test scores to promote their own reputations. Politicians touted as senatorial or Presidential material drop out of contention for high office because of scandals, one out of every two couples trade their marriage papers for divorce papers. If that isn't bad enough, according to a recent survey of American ethics, "two in every three Americans today believe there is nothing wrong with telling a lie; only 31% believe that honesty is the best policy."[1]

I am sure that readers have noticed that in the previous chapter we dealt extensively with the ambiguous state of ethics in our pluralistic world, without focusing entirely on issues of business ethics per se. However, this quotation from the April 6, 1992, issue of *Industry Week* magazine, the lead-in to an article on integrity in business, reminds us again that business ethics are a reflection of the general ethical climate of society. In fact, that same magazine, some months earlier, reported results of their business ethics survey that serve to underscore that point. Among the reasons given for unethical conduct in business are the sad state of ethics in society as a whole and the lack of ethical education at all levels of schooling.[2] Clearly we need, then, to continue paying attention to the ethical orientation of the cultural context in which business operates, as well as the underlying problems of moral authority that contribute to the ethical ambiguity and moral cynicism so prevalent in much of our society.

As we noted in chapter 1 and have spelled out further since, the general prejudice of secular rationalism in our culture, which resists the influence of religion in morality, has had its impact on business ethics as well, perpetuating a long-standing dualism between the sacred and the secular, a dualism that consigns faith to private life and anoints reason as the arbiter of ethical issues in business, politics, and other "secular" matters. The church, for its part, we also observed, has reinforced this dualism by frequently opting out of involvement in secular struggles—as we shall see, often on theological grounds—and by showing its disdain for business through neglect or even hostility. These dualistic forces are at the heart of the shareability gap. Pluralism is a sign that the hegemony of secular rationalism is breaking down, just as the authority of religion has been eroded by secularization. If we cannot find a way out of this age-old dualism wherein the concerns of religious faith can engage the ethical impulses of the so-called secular sphere, we may end up with moral cynicism in an age of relativity.

CAN WE TALK? A MODEL FOR DIALOGUE

When comedian Joan Rivers says, "Can we talk?" it is, of course, a humorous rhetorical question. But for us it is a real question. The "work of faith," the vocation of the Christian in business, we have said, is to *speak*, to express the hope within us through bringing the insights of faith to bear on the ethical questions of life in business.

Most of the business leaders with whom I spoke on these matters believed that it should be possible for the contributions of religious faith to have a hearing in the precincts of business. All thought it would not be easy to develop this process, and no one was very clear about how one might go about it. One retired executive of a nationally known food corporation felt that, although there is more awareness and training in ethics today, sharing one's faith convictions was easier years ago when the corporation was smaller and more personal, when everyone knew everyone else. In the larger and more impersonal corporate world, we do not rock the boat with a personal agenda. However, another business leader, the president of a large national insurance corporation, said that, when companies discourage the influence of religious perspectives within the ranks, they are simply denying the pluralism that they know exists and that they pretend to affirm. It is his conviction that business can and should provide forums wherein employees and business leaders can work toward consensus in a situation of diversity, where all are respected for their particular contributions, even though no one perspective may be honored above all others. In any case, we need a model for such dialogue that enables Christians in business to "talk" and be heard and understood.

Although Michael J. Perry's purpose is to examine the relationship of religious morality to politics, his book *Love and Power* is of special interest to us because of the dialogical method he develops as a proposal for how that relationship might work. I want to suggest that this method holds promise for our investigation of the dialogue between Christian moral insight and the ethics of business. A Catholic and a law professor at Northwestern University, Perry sees the cultural challenge to the expression of religious morality and, indeed, morality in general in terms much the same as we have set forth. The opening sentence of his first chapter sets the context: "The United States, like many other societies, is morally pluralistic. No one set of beliefs about how it is good or fitting for human beings to live their lives prevails in American society."[3]

Perry believes that religion should have a voice in the moral shape of political life, a legitimate voice among the many voices that make up our diverse society. Consequently, one of the "dear enemies" Perry attacks is the notion that there can and ought to be a "neutral politics" in which only undisputed claims about the human good can be admitted into the discourse of public policy making. Involved in this view are positions like that of political philosopher Thomas Nagel, who argues that political neutrality requires that only those claims regarding the human good and the common good are permissible in public policy debate that can be justified by "impartial" or "objective" premises of "common critical rationality" and consideration of "evidence that can be shared."[4]

For Perry the idea of a neutral politics along these lines is impossibly restrictive.[5] Political neutrality of this sort unfairly excludes the input of a rich variety of cultural and religious communities by drawing lines that can no longer be drawn. Moreover, the insights of this combined diversity are needed for a fuller picture and for understanding in a pluralistic culture. In the final analysis, no neutral language exists for the discussion of ethical concerns in public policy formation or any other sector of life.[6] Indeed, I would add that an emerging feature of contemporary pluralism is to make respect for the integrity of various views and particular perspectives an ethical imperative of our tradition of egalitarian justice. This makes the maintenance of neutral zones of ethical discourse increasingly indefensible *on ethical grounds.*

Perry himself believes that we have enough shareable standards of human rights in our constitutional tradition to create a community of moral discourse in which people have a sufficient fund of common convictions about the human good to understand one another, despite their cultural diversity.[7] However, out of respect for that diversity, the dialogue of ethical deliberation in the public forum will need to be *ecumenical.*

The analogy is with the ecumenical movement of the Christian churches in which, Perry observes, the diversity of beliefs and traditions within Christianity proved to be a stimulus to ecumenical dialogue and ecumenical theology.[8] To be "ecumenical" is to be universal or inclusive and respectful of all viewpoints. In ecumenical dialogue the dialogue partners participate with a commitment to understand and appreciate one another's views and to seek common grounds of belief wherever possible. While there is an openness to change and to find new formulations more congenial to unity, it is understood that participants will maintain the integrity of their own outlooks and traditions.

Perry discusses a number of virtues and attitudes essential to participation in ecumenical dialogue. They are, in effect, rules of the game as well as traits of character. Several of these, such as the ability to understand the arguments of others, readiness to seek out all the relevant facts, respect, honesty, and sincerity, are all fairly obvious requirements. Two essential attitudes that he mentions deserve some special attention, however. Engaging in ecumenical dialogue means embracing *fallibilism* and *pluralism*. Taking these two concepts in reverse order, let me first simply quote Perry on pluralism before taking up a more thorough discussion of fallibilism:

> To be a pluralist, in the sense relevant here, is to understand that a morally pluralistic context, with its attendant variety of ways of life, can often be a more fertile source of deepening moral insight—in particular, a more fertile soil for dialogue leading to deepening moral insight—than can a monistic context. Ways of life different from our own can test our beliefs about what ways of life are good for human beings and, moreover, fuel our efforts to imagine better ways of life.[9]

The attitude of fallibilism is allied to the pluralist attitude just described. To be a fallibilist is simply to have the capacity and willingness to be self-critical. In serious dialogue our own cherished views are often challenged in substance or in form. Our interpretations of things are challenged by different interpretations, and we sometimes face the prospect that our strongly held opinions are based on an inadequate or even erroneous grasp of the truth of things. The pluralist openness to the possibility that ecumenical dialogue may lead to better results than simply talking with others of like mind is enhanced by the capacity for self-criticism. Self-criticism is a necessary antidote to the tendencies of institutions, religious or secular, to become entrenched. Perry says it well: "A religious community no less than a political one—especially a religious bureaucracy no less than a political one—can tend to absolutize itself and, so, can need reminding 'that even basic principles are subject to revision as human understanding grows.' Authentic religious faith and the virtue of fallibilism are intimately connected."[10]

These last words on fallibilism serve to underscore a key feature of ecumenical dialogue that should be clear by now. In such dialogues no one holds a privileged position, and all participate on a level playing field. For some Christian traditions, this can be a very threatening state of affairs. Rigid dogmatism on behalf of one's beliefs makes participation in dialogue impossible. Indeed, such rigidity can survive only in the isolation provided by maintaining the very dualistic separation of sacred and secular that we seek to overcome. However, as Perry's words suggest, there are in the Christian tradition rich resources for cultivating the capacity of self-criticism and openness to change that should, in fact, enable the Christian community to provide leadership in this regard.

The Reformation is marked by the rediscovery of the theological truth that we are all hopelessly mired in sin and that we are accounted worthy and acceptable in God's sight only by the grace of God in Jesus Christ and our faith in that promise, not by any virtues we possess or works we have done. This central doctrine of the Christian faith is our key to interpreting life and understanding its meaning. The great modern theologian Paul Tillich referred to this as the Protestant Principle. This principle provides a critical perspective on the cultural tendencies toward the *profane* and the *demonic*. The profane is the elimination of God from our account of life and reality. The demonic is making absolute what is only finite and conditional.[11]

The Protestant Principle, reflecting its underlying conviction that we live in a fallen world utterly dependent on God's grace, helps the Christian community to see that it belongs in dialogue in the realm of the secular as a counterpoint to the profane. But it also teaches the church that it must be ready for self-criticism and reform in the give-and-take of that involvement. If it is not, it can itself become demonic, claiming absolute authority for the form of its traditions and the practice of its institutions. However, if the church rightly understands that its own existence is grounded not in being right but in being forgiven and accepted by God despite sin, it is wonderfully free for self-critical reflection and for honest dialogue.[12]

This freedom in the gospel breeds the kind of openness that we also associate with agape, or love of neighbor. Perry sees the connection between loving as Christ has loved us and the imperative to engage in dialogue. "I can hardly love the Other—the *real* other, in all her particularity—unless I listen to her and, in listening, gain in knowledge of her, of who she truly is and what she needs or desires; and unless, having listened, I then respond to her."[13]

ECONOMIC LIFE AND THE REIGN OF GOD

As noted earlier, Perry's proposal for ecumenical dialogue challenges the existing dualism between the sacred and the secular in the political arena. This is also the context of Thiemann's advocacy of a public theology, which was discussed in the previous chapter. I have not dealt directly with the historical, cultural, and theological roots of the modern gulf between religion and politics. Rather, I have simply gleaned from both thinkers those lessons and ideas that I believe can be applied fruitfully to our concern for the work of faith in the ethics of business.

However, the challenge to secular thought, whether in Thiemann's public theology or Perry's dialogical proposal, is one that rests on certain theological assumptions that the Christian community has a genuine mission in public life and public policy formation. Historically, the church has been divided over the manner in which it properly relates to the institutions of political life. It has, perhaps, been even more ambivalent, if not simply standoffish, when it comes to relating constructively to the institutions of economic life.

In his book *God the Economist,* M. Douglas Meeks observes: "The church sometimes thinks and lives as if God were outside the pale of economy...."[14] For Meeks the incipient dualism of this isolation of the church from being involved in the issues of the economic order and the institutions of economic life is in large measure due to its capitulation to a secularized view of economics, which was a part of the general process of secularization since the Enlightenment. From Adam Smith to the latter part of the nineteenth century, the development of economics, as purely a mathematical and mechanistic science that revealed a universal self-regulating economic system, served to eliminate any need for dealing with God when dealing with matters of the economy. And Christian theology, both liberal and conservative, dutifully accepted this account of economic reality and restricted its claims to the sphere of private life and personal spirituality.[15]

If we are to move from dualism to dialogue, we need some kind of fix on a theological understanding of the nature and role of economic institutions and the manner in which Christian witness is authentically involved. If the prospect of ecumenical dialogue in a pluralistic world challenges the institutions of secular life, in general, and of business, in particular, to rethink their approach to ethics, it challenges the church to review the dualistic tendencies of its theology in relation to those institutions. Such an undertaking could itself be the subject of a long study.[16] For the present, we shall simply have to provide enough theological guidance to set our compass for the rest of the announced task.

We already have some clues for our direction. In chapter 2 we built a Christian understanding of vocation on biblical and Reformation themes. There we asserted that Christian identity in vocation is characterized by freedom for service and that service in the occupations or stations of life is a channel that God establishes for the providential care of humanity and the world. This service of our vocation is an integral part of our Christian call to witness, and that witness in service and in ethics is an expression of our hope for the world in the gospel promise of God's coming reign, revealed in Christ. These key points are our jumping-off points for the work now before us.

In Luther's thought the exercise of our vocation through the occupations of life or, as he also called them, "offices" of life was understood within the larger framework of the "orders" that God establishes as the ongoing institutions of divine love for the creation and its basic needs of sustenance. Our offices or occupations in life are functions of an order and those divinely devised orders include marriage, parenthood, education, and government.[17] The manifold institutions of economic life logically belong here as part of the array of orders that serve the common good. Among these we would list corporations, businesses both small and large, markets, labor, and finance. These various entities, arrangements, and forces are always in a state of development, of course, but they are, theologically speaking, to be guided and judged in that development by their effectiveness in serving the common good in accordance with the divine plan.[18] (The "historical" and "developmental" character of economic institutions and other "orders" is a point we will take up later.)

The orders, as institutions of divine providence within which we exercise our vocation in our offices, were subsumed under God's "left-hand" mode of governance in Luther's scheme of things. Luther saw God's rule as expressed in two modes: the right hand and the left hand. God's right-hand rule (the kingdom of the right) is that which God exerts over the hearts of believers through the gospel. The left-hand rule is expressed through the orders and offices that God establishes for our good. Here the "civil use" of God's law governs and guides these historical institutions. We have discussed the law of God in its judging function. In the civil use of the law, the word of God provides ethical direction and the foundations of civil and criminal law.[19]

Luther's vision of God's two modes of governance was born out of his response to a problem of his day. Luther saw that church authorities were meddling in the affairs of government, and government authorities were meddling in the affairs of the church. These power struggles were creating distortions of both church and state to the detriment of the faith and

of justice in society. Luther's two realms doctrine was an effort to mitigate the confusions of authorities by saying that in God's plan the governing authorities should stick to their vocation of governing in matters
of civil concern and the church authorities should stick to the business of
the church and proclaim the gospel. As such, it was a breakthrough for
needed reform; by providing the concepts of vocation and orders, it gave
theological significance to all of life's work.

However, there is an irony in the history of Luther's two realms
thought since the time of the Reformation. Although Luther advocated
a needed social, political, and ecclesiastical reform, which was successful
in many respects, the formulation of two realms eventually led much of
the church away from involvement in social and political affairs. The
inertia of Luther's twofold formulation carried many theologians and
church leaders into a dualistic interpretation of his thought. It was easy
to see the notion of two modes of divine governance as two distinct
spheres of reality: the secular on the left and the sacred on the right, or
this world versus the world to come. Once we start to dichotomize in
this fashion, it is a short step to saying that the church should stick to the
sacred and stay out of secular matters entirely. Christians should be good
citizens and honest businesspeople, to be sure, but this is something one
does as an individual. Thus, people in government, business, and all
walks of life are left wondering how to connect faith and life with little
help from the church in doing so.

Certainly there are strong elements in Luther's thought that contributed to the dualism that resulted from his teaching. However, it was
Luther's purpose to deal with abuses of power by reminding certain
leaders to stick to their proper roles. He did not want to suggest that the
church and the world had nothing to talk about and that the church
should steer clear of all involvement in the affairs of government or business. As Gustaf Wingren, the great Lutheran theologian, has pointed
out, the two realms were linked together in Luther's system because
both modes of governance are expressions of God's love, and our
response is, in our public and private lives, one of love for the neighbor.[20]
This is the living out of our vocation as we have seen. The civil use of
the law provides ethical and legal direction for Christians and non-
Christians alike, but Christians appropriate it in the freedom of the
gospel as a vehicle of love for the neighbor: "It is the neighbor who
stands at the center of Luther's ethics.... Vocation and law benefit the
neighbor, as does love born of faith.... Love born of faith and the Spirit
effects a complete breakthrough of the boundary between the two kingdoms, the wall of partition between heaven and earth, as did God's
incarnation in Christ."[21]

This linkage between the two realms or "breakthrough of the boundary between kingdoms" that Wingren has observed is important because
it helps to mitigate the dualism that has historically plagued us. It also
connects this point in the discussion with an earlier point we noted about
the reign of God. In chapter 2 we saw that the service of love and the
ethics of love are for Christians a witness to the hope that is within them
for the coming reign of God. Acts and advocacy in love for the neighbor
are anticipations of the promise of the coming reign of God when the
values we seek in love for the neighbor will be realized in their fullness.
This carries forward the point that love active in all facets of our vocation links the two realms together and breaks down any false barriers
between the two. But it also adds a new accent in identifying the ethics
of love as an anticipation of the coming reign of God.

Rediscovery of the nature and dynamics of the biblical vision of the
coming reign of God in contemporary theology has been a powerful
influence in drawing the Christian community more deeply and actively
into the concerns of the whole of life, not just spiritual concerns. To put
the matter all too briefly, when we recognize that the dominion of God
Jesus proclaimed and secured in his victory over sin and death is a reign
in which all of creation is redeemed and fulfilled in its perfection, we
then recognize that all of creation is our concern.[22] Care for all aspects of
life is integral to our witness that Christ's promise of the reign of God is
a promise for the redemption of all things. Needless to say, from this
vantage point, a dualistic approach that separates the concerns of
Christian faith and love from the issues of life in politics, business, or
other "secular" pursuits is hardly tenable.

Before we proclaim victory over dualism, however, we need to realize that there is a certain sense in which a measure of dualism is
inevitable. We live in a fallen world where sin continues to hold sway in
the hearts of individuals, as well as in the systems and institutions sinful
people have shaped within the "orders." One of the major purposes of
Luther's two realms doctrine was to point the finger of truth at that reality and help us to recognize that, even though the left-hand realm is of
divine origin, it is in the hands of sinful people and constantly subject to
the judgment of the law as well as the guidance of the civil use of the
law. Institutions cannot claim absolute authority in any area of human
affairs. This is one of the insights Tillich picked up in formulating the
Protestant Principle. Consequently, we will always encounter a duality
between what is and what ought to be, between things as they are in
their present ambiguous blend of good and evil and things as they are
promised to be in the arrival of God's coming reign.

Luther sometimes referred to the orders as "orders of creation." Helmut Thielicke has criticized this nomenclature as giving the false impression that the institutions of life are the way God created them to be.[23] I think Thielicke is correct in light of the reality of evil and Luther's own best insights. Consequently, I would prefer to think of the orders as "orders of vocation," providential structures of worldly arrangements within which we are called to live out our vocation of service. Alternatively or additionally, we might well call the orders "orders of anticipation" to stress that it is within these historical institutions that our striving for the good is a way to anticipate the promise of God's future and lift up a message of hope in the midst of ambiguity.

Here, then, theologically speaking, is where we locate the meaning and significance of business; it is an order of vocation and anticipation. This means that the Christian community is called to be constructively involved in the affairs of economic life. It will do so by lifting up a message of affirmation for the role of business in promoting the common good. It will do so by lifting up a message of hope in the values it advocates. It will do so also in lifting up the judgment of the law against the evils of abusive power and greed that cause so much suffering. The church is entrusted with the word of both law and gospel and, in a state of anticipation where realism and hope cohabit, both words are needed.

For Christians, ethics in business will be motivated by the gospel as an expression of service in love and witness to hope through vocation, but for those outside the faith the motive may be the coercion of the civil and criminal law, the conviction that ethics is good for business, the pressure of public opinion, or an admirable degree of humanistic good will. In any case, the Christian witness in the ethics of business will not "Christianize" business, however positive its influence, and the engagement in dialogue that we advocate will not always prove to be fruitful. (The impediments to dialogue are not simply intellectual; they have to do with human perversity as well.) The ambiguity of life in a state of anticipation prevents us from the naive optimism that with a little (or even a lot of) moral effort we can somehow create a progressively ideal state of affairs.

Placing business in the theological category of an order of vocation and anticipation also helps us see that it exists in an interactive relationship with other orders for the benefit of the overall good. The institutions of economic life and the economy are not a law unto themselves; they act and are acted upon by other dimensions of God's providence: government, education, marriage and family life, and stewardship of natural resources, to add one that has yet to be mentioned.[24] This interactive relationship came out clearly with respect to the relationship of business and government at a recent international conference on business ethics of which I was a part. Former U. S. senator Richard S. Schweiker, now president of the American Council of Life Insurance, observed that, while capitalism has been reborn in our day, it is still on trial. It needs to show its capability to take leadership in areas where it can move faster than governments, such as laying the foundations for international business ethics in an increasingly global economy. At the same time, it needs the help of government to take leadership in areas where government is best suited, such as regulations on behalf of the environment, a good example of an area where self-regulation and competition do not always appear congenial to one another.[25]

Both economic institutions and church institutions are tempted to seek security. When one is comfortable with things as they are, there is little impetus to change, and change is easily seen as a threat. The dualism that has kept the church and business relatively disengaged offers a certain sense of comfort and security, whereas involvement with one another seems risky and even dangerous. As Meeks has put it, "Compulsion to security leaves no energy for imagining a different, more just world."[26] The dynamic of the promise of God's coming reign is to challenge that drive toward security and offer in its stead the freedom of hope to risk embracing the good in love.

DIALOGUE: COMMUNICATION AND STRATEGY

Thus far we have said that dialogue can help to overcome dualism. We have stressed that this dialogical endeavor is a crucial dimension of bridging the shareability gap and thereby finding a way to give voice to Christian perspectives on ethics in business. Our discussion has been about communication.

Dialogue is also a strategy for creating change. Most of the time, communication about ethics has its strategic dimension of attempting to be persuasive on behalf of certain moral values. Better communication leads to better understanding, better understanding leads to more persuasive arguments, and more persuasive arguments lead to better possibilities for change. That is roughly the formula. However, although the strategic thrust may be inherent in ethical dialogue, the dialogical approach to change may be chosen deliberately as an alternative to confrontation or coercion. An episode in my own experience helps me to develop this point.

More than a decade ago I was privileged to participate in a dialogue between church and industry that revolved around the infant formula controversy, one of the big issues at that time. The industry in question was Ross Laboratories, a division of Abbott Laboratories and the manufacturer of the infant formula Similac. The controversy over the marketing of infant formula revolved around its promotion in Third World countries. The primary target was the Nestlé corporation because Nestlé had the largest share of that market and was thought to be a major culprit in its marketing practices.

Although Ross had the largest domestic sales of all formulas, it had only small markets in the Third World and was considered by industry critics to be among the more responsible corporations. Nonetheless, they were still included in the attack and felt the pressure of being part of an industry under fire. Because church-related organizations like the Interfaith Center on Corporate Responsibility were in the forefront of the protest and there was broad participation by churches in the boycott of Nestlé products, Ross officials were interested in a dialogue with church leaders. A group of us, representing the Methodist, Lutheran, Episcopal, and Catholic communions, agreed to oblige and, with that, launched a dialogue that lasted for nearly three years.[27]

From the point of view of the critics, the multinational and local corporations manufacturing infant formula for sale in developing countries were guilty of promoting bottle-feeding over breast-feeding, through irresponsible marketing and advertising, in areas where use of formula is unsafe. In conditions of severe poverty, where water is unclean, hygiene is inadequate, refrigeration is nonexistent, and illiteracy is widespread, the use of bottle-feeding and formula is dangerous: People who cannot read cannot read directions; dirty water contaminates formula; lack of money and knowledge prompts people to dilute formula in order to make it stretch. The consequences of such factors were babies who were malnourished or suffered illnesses like gastroenteritis. Many died.

The sort of advertising practices singled out by the critics associated formula with the health care profession in such a way as to give the impression, directly or indirectly, that bottle-feeding was superior. Such techniques, the protesters asserted, easily lured mothers away from a safer, more nutritious course of breast-feeding.

Neither party in the dialogue believed that the life and health of babies should be risked for profit. The issue turned around whether and how formula could be marketed ethically, if at all.

From our dialogue partners in the industry, we learned to make distinctions between the differing practices of the companies in the market. We learned to appreciate that the situations in all poverty areas are not the same and that a variety of social and cultural forces, as well as different traditional practices in feeding babies, affect the demand for formula and the degree to which it is a singular hazard. In summary, we learned that the situation was more complicated than it appeared to be and that the Christian community, for its part, needed to be more attentive to the ethical fairness of its own criticism of industry ethics. Clearly there was culpability on the part of some corporations, and dramatic changes were needed. At the same time, protests that seem unfair in not fully representing all facets of reality offer little incentive for change; they inspire defensiveness and resistance.

From our little ecumenical church group, the corporation leaders learned something of the reasoning behind the ethical challenges being mounted. We were able to articulate and develop further the specifically Christian impulses involved in the ethical concerns being voiced by church groups and leaders. They, in turn, shared their impressions of the message they thought was coming through from the church, namely, a wholesale denunciation of capitalism and the free enterprise system. This was a highly emotional crossroad at which the dialogue could easily have derailed if we had not found the openness required to forgo stereotyping each other's views.

During our dialogue period, the World Health Organization (WHO) and UNICEF were jointly sponsoring an international code to govern the marketing of infant formula. As preliminary drafts of the code were made public, we worked with the people at Ross on their emerging response and were permitted in the process to be party to their internal memoranda.

The dialogue included some confrontation and challenge, as well as analysis, ethical deliberation, and a search for better understanding. One example serves to illustrate. Ross was committed to public advocacy of breast-feeding but also maintained that formula could be marketed ethically to meet the needs of babies when breast-feeding was not possible or sufficient. One could hardly argue with that. However, beyond that claim, the company also developed the theme of freedom of choice for women who were entering the workforce or had other life situations that made breast-feeding difficult. Freedom of choice has a strong appeal in our tradition, but we were forced to point out that freedom of choice is bounded by the impact one's choices will have on the well-being of others. Leaving that choice open to those who cannot make it responsibly is ethically irresponsible unless every effort is made to reduce risk to infants.

What can be said of the outcomes of this extensive dialogue? I have given only a brief sketch of but a few of its features. However, perhaps enough has been reported that we can move to the question of outcomes. First of all, with respect to dialogue as a method of communication, there were two basic results.

1. We discovered that there are values inherent in the process that

make dialogue ethically significant in itself and more than just a technique. Dialogue embodies respect for persons by assuming, of necessity, that one's dialogue partner is capable of being honest and fair. Rather than putting them on the defensive, they have a chance to be their best.

2. The dialogical values just mentioned created a situation of trust in which we were able to find an adequate language by which to bring the contributions of faith into conversation with the logic of business and its ethical concerns. In the process, both partners expanded their conceptual frameworks and vocabularies to encompass each other's worlds. (This is a necessary precondition to developing intelligible and shareable grounds for ethical authority in a pluralistic world.)

Second, as a strategy for creating change, this adventure in dialogue is much more difficult to evaluate. To begin with, there were so many political and social forces already at work in this international controversy that our small-scale venture with one company was hardly in a position to be a decisive factor. Nonetheless, some things can be said.

1. If we had hoped for some industry leadership from Ross in giving at least a qualified assent to the WHO-UNICEF code, the dialogue was a strategic failure. Ross lined up with the rest of the industry in supporting our government's opposition to the code. Still, this may not have been a failure of our dialogue but a failure of the confrontational politics, which initiated the code's development and failed in the process to acknowledge industry's compliance with most of the code's provisions.

2. The dialogue did enable us to move beyond issues of ethical sanctions to discussing more positive steps industry could take in addressing the health crises of poverty zones. This emphasis on proactive social responsibility is a dimension of ethical concern that dialogue can get at more readily than confrontation.

In the final analysis, the most tangible outcome of this experiment was the formation of the Council for Ethics in Economics, which during the past decade has fostered continuing dialogue on a variety of ethical issues. We will look more closely at the work of that organization in the final chapter. For the present we need simply observe that the successes of the council in attracting both business and religious participation and support for its program are a testimony to the trust-building effects of dialogue.

This kind of dialogue is a step away from the sort of ethical dialogue, inclusive of religious perspectives, that is internal to the corporate culture and carried forward by the corporate community itself. Nonetheless, it is adjunct to the development of inclusive dialogue in the formation of corporate cultures, and it helps us envision what such a dialogue might look like.

5

BEYOND THE MORAL MINIMUM

Attention to ethics could mean smaller fines and could even keep one out of jail. That is what a growing number of business leaders are coming to recognize as the result of a recent government initiative. According to a report in the business ethics periodical *Ethikos*, the federal organizational sentencing guidelines issued by the U.S. Sentencing Commission in November 1991 provide for reduced fines when organizations guilty of violating the law have had in place a program to prevent and detect such violations.

> As the Commission sees it, an "effective" compliance program is a fairly major undertaking, generally involving codes of conduct, ethics training sessions, disciplinary systems, auditing and monitoring efforts, mechanisms to encourage employees to report violations without fear of retribution, and proper accountability for the program as a whole. Corporations that fail to adopt such measures—and spurn the government's invitation to become partners—risk the possibility of devastating fines.[1]

At least one respected business ethics consultant I know has reported that the consulting business has picked up noticeably since word of the commission's offer has spread.

There are a variety of motives for trying to do the right thing and for taking ethics seriously. Among them are fear of the consequences for not doing so and the pragmatic conviction that, overall, it pays to be ethical. The U.S. Sentencing Commission's offer appeals to both of these kinds of motives. Others do not need that enticement; they are committed to high ethical standards simply because it's right or because it contributes to the greater good. Whatever the case, the variety of motives we can observe alerts us to the fact that consideration of motive is part of any ethics discussion. Beliefs about the importance of motive and the kind of motive that is morally praiseworthy may be the very feature that distinguishes one approach to ethics from others.

It is arguable that the motive of love is that feature of the Christian ethic that, more than any other, distinguishes it from other ethical systems or outlooks. Certainly chapter 2 showed that the love that emanates from the experience of being loved by God in Christ is at the vital center of our vocation of service and witness. As we bring the theme of Christian love or agape (the Greek word used in the New Testament) into dialogue with the ethics of business, we need to observe, first of all, that love has to do with motive.

FORMED BY LOVE: THE EXTRA MILE

In Matthew 5:41 we read: "and if anyone forces you to go one mile, go also the second mile." At the time of Jesus, the Romans had apparently legalized an ancient Near Eastern tradition of commandeering people to perform services. This they often imposed on Jewish citizens. For example, Simon was commandeered to carry Jesus' cross (Mark 15:21). The command to go a mile referred to in Matthew 5:41 is an allusion to this practice of commandeering. Jesus' counsel is that you should go beyond what the law requires; go the extra mile.[2]

As we look at the background of this familiar saying, we begin to get a glimpse of the nature of love as an attitude or orientation of character. The follower of Christ is to focus on the needs of the other person without concern for his or her own prerogatives or rights. Rather than protecting one's own interest by doing no more than the law requires, love does more than the law requires and thereby demonstrates freedom from the law in the interest of the neighbor.

The same insight applies to other statements in the immediate context that exhort us not to resist the evildoer and to turn the other cheek (v. 39). In other words, do not seek the legal recompense provided by the existing law of "an eye for an eye and a tooth for a tooth" (v. 38), but be concerned instead for the well-being of the neighbor.

This is the kind of self-giving love that we witness in Jesus. His focus is not on his own rightful demands or prerogatives but on our salvation. Having experienced his self-giving love in the sacrifice of the cross, we are moved to the same love in concern for the good of the neighbor. Freed by God's loving acceptance of us in Christ, we are free to be for the neighbor. Herein is the motive of the love ethic, as we are formed in love by the grace of God. No one captures this life of love in Christ better than Paul, who admonishes us to be the people of love God creates us to be:

> If then there is any encouragement in Christ, any consolation from love, any sharing in the Spirit, any compassion and sympathy, make my joy complete: be of the same mind, having the same love, being in full accord and of one mind. Do nothing from selfish ambition or conceit, but in

humility regard others as better than yourselves. Let each of you look not
to your own interests, but to the interests of others. Let the same mind be
in you that was in Christ Jesus,

> who, though he was in the form
> of God,
> did not regard equality with God
> as something to be exploited,
> but emptied himself,
> taking the form of a slave,
> being born in human likeness.
> And being found in human form,
> he humbled himself
> and became obedient to the point of death—
> even death on a cross. (Philippians 2:1-8)

As we probe the freely given love of Christ in which we are formed
and the ethical motive of self-giving concern for the neighbor that it
produces, we sense that there is already implied some hint of what love
entails as a guide to ethical behavior or ethical obligation.

INFORMED BY LOVE:
BEYOND THE MORAL MINIMUM

Most of us are familiar with the maxim "above all, do no harm." It has
been frequently associated with the tradition that lies behind the Hippo-
cratic oath to which physicians subscribe, but this is uncertain.[3] Whatever its origins, it is generally considered to be a succinct statement of
the "moral minimum."

In one of the most widely used textbooks on business ethics, Richard
De George observes that this injunction to do no harm spells out the primary moral obligation corporations have in matters of environmental
concern and product safety.[4] De George rejects what he calls the "myth
of amoral business," a view that regards corporations as legal entities, at
best, to which we cannot attribute moral capacities or obligations as we
can to individuals. However, although he believes that corporations, as
human organizations, are susceptible to moral evaluation, he does concede that they are different from individual moral agents. As organizational entities, they lack a personal center and a conscience, except as
reflected in this leadership. Consequently, he seems to say that the only
moral injunction we can consistently place upon corporations—in general, not only in environmental protection and product safety matters—
is the moral minimum to do no harm. Given the nature of business entities and their narrowly defined purposes, it is hard to say when they have
an obligation to go beyond that minimum. And given the impersonal

character of an organization, it is impossible to think of a corporation acting out of moral motives.[5]

We need some further discussion of De George's influential views on the moral status of corporations, but already our brief look at agape suggests that contrast and tension between the love ethic and the ethics of organizational life are in the offing. Let us first look further at the New Testament teaching on love and the way it informs us or gives direction for ethical decision.

Jesus' encouragement to go the extra mile already tells us that love is geared to going beyond the moral minimum, beyond what the law requires or prohibits, in meeting the needs of the neighbor. This self-giving and generous character of love is even more sharply defined by the additional disclosure that no one is excluded as a potential recipient of our love. In the same context of the Sermon on the Mount where we met the extra mile saying, we hear Jesus command in Matthew 5:43-44: "'you have heard that it was said, "you shall love your neighbor and hate your enemy." But I say to you, Love your enemies and pray for those who persecute you'" (see also Luke 6:27-28). No one is disqualified, not even one's enemy. As the love of God is without conditions, so our love is to be unconditional as well. There is no requirement of reciprocity governing the expression of agape and no criteria of worthiness by which one is judged deserving of either God's love or our love: "the command to love one's enemies suggests that such love would mean acknowledging their presence and the bond that exists between oneself and them by virtue of *sharing together in the beneficence and mercy of God.*"[6]

The "enemy" in this command of Jesus means, first of all, those considered outsiders with respect to being counted among God's people. Jesus' ministry to the outcasts, the sick, the downtrodden and despised, and even to Gentiles exemplifies this embrace of all people, even those rejected by the religious community. When the words "pray for those who persecute you" are added, we realize that even our *personal* enemies who seek to harm us are included. The commandment to love calls us to seek peace and reconciliation with those who oppose us, even though this drives us beyond the moral minimum and beyond what most would consider the limit of our obligations.[7] The example of Jesus—hanging on the cross and yet praying to God to forgive those who crucified him—is the picture that comes immediately into focus.

The all-inclusive, unconditional nature of love reinforces our understanding of its motivation as that of self-giving care for the neighbor, unalloyed by any necessity that the neighbor be lovable. Victor Paul Furnish puts it: "And love is not guided in its course, like an antiballistic missile, by something inherently attractive in its object. It is empowered and guided, rather, by it own inherent rightness as a response to human need."[8]

Understanding the all-inclusive character of love not only deepens our understanding of our formation in love but informs us on the direction of our ethical choices. Love will obviously go beyond the moral minimum in its orientation to matters of human need. In that commitment, love will logically follow a course of advocacy for equalitarian justice in which no one is excluded or discriminated against with respect to essential goods and opportunities by virtue of who or what they are. Furthermore, outreach to all, regardless of who they are, reveals a goal of love that is reflective of the goal of God's love revealed in the work of Christ: to bring about reconciliation and community with God and with one another.

The goal of reconciliation and community is evident in many places in the Bible, but, to keep matters in the context of Jesus' teaching on love, it is perhaps most clear in Luke's version of the love commandment, to which is appended the parable of the Good Samaritan. In this familiar story, the hated, outcast Samaritan comes to the aid of the hapless Jew and thereby makes the point that love breaks down all the barriers that divide people. Jesus tells the parable in connection with the command to love the neighbor because, in this Lukan account, he is confronted by the question of a lawyer, "And who is my neighbor?" One might say that the lawyer was seeking a definition of *neighbor* in order to determine what the minimum moral requirement was. The parable makes clear that *neighbor* is an all-inclusive term and that those who are shaped by love do not even pause to ask questions like "Who is my neighbor?"[9]

LOVE, BENEFICENCE, AND BUSINESS

New Testament scholar Robert Guelich points out that Jesus' teachings about going the extra mile, turning the other cheek, and loving one's enemies are all reflective of a new state of affairs that Jesus has ushered in. Such love is possible only because Jesus, the Christ, has brought in the reign of God and, by grace, has created a new people of faith and hope in the promise of that coming dominion.[10]

The resurrection victory over sin and death reveals the future of a dominion in which things are brought to fulfillment and wholeness. In faith and hope in that promise, we are set free to love as we have been loved. These observations square nicely with our earlier remarks about how love is at the heart of the Christian community's witness of anticipation. In our vocation of witness, the service of love to the neighbor, in its quest for the values of the promised reign of God, expresses the hope that is within it for the fulfillment of those values. As such, the ethic of love is an ethic of anticipation, anticipating the fulfillment of God's promise for the future by seeking the promised values in the present.

In that it is grounded in faith and hope in the promise of God in Jesus Christ and can hardly be understood apart from that connection, there is a real sense in which the motive and direction, the attitude and action of agape can be the possession of only the Christian community.

Having said this, we should be prepared for someone to say, "Wait a minute! I've seen non-Christians provide outstanding examples of the kind of behavior Christians associate with love. I've also seen a lot of professed Christians who are hardly shining examples of morality. What's so special about Christian love as an ethical ideal? And, most of all, what's so special about Christians?"

If we take the last question first, we have to concede that our imaginary challenger has a point. Christians are "not yet" people, just as the love they try to show is an anticipation and not a fulfillment of the ideal. Sin remains a reality, within the Christian community as well as throughout the world. Even the combined witness of the best the whole church has to offer does not add up to a perfect love. At the same time, there is also much evidence of the Spirit's work in the lives of believers, forming them in love and moving them to loving actions. The Christian witness in love is fragmentary and incomplete, just as the general moral landscape of our world is ambiguous. Moreover, if the performance of Christians does not always seem distinctive, it also seems to be the case that other ethical systems foster ideals that strongly resemble the Christian version of love without being tied to that faith.

While some may challenge the distinctive claims of the love ethic, others have said it is too special, too bound to the presuppositions of the Christian faith. If love is taken seriously, it is too radical to function in a fallen world where evil must be resisted and legal recompense is needed to ensure justice. For a long time, many have maintained, Christians and non-Christians alike, that the ethic of love is for individuals to pursue in their personal lives. In politics, government, and business, another standard needs to operate, one more oriented to the strict rule of law. Therefore, to motivate business to pursue a higher moral standard by offering lighter sentences to those who institute company ethics programs is not only more realistic; it is also more appropriate to the way business operates most effectively, that is, pragmatically rather than idealistically.

Whether we favor the view that the Christian love ethic is not special enough to be distinctive, the view that it is too special to be practical, or neither, we need some clarity on the relation of love ethics to ethics in general and to business ethics in particular. Such clarity is important because the issues we will be dealing with from now on are issues of going the extra mile or going beyond the moral minimum. We need to know if there is in the ethics of business a place for a contribution from the logic of Christian love.

For me, it is helpful to begin this inquiry by looking at the principle of beneficence. Beneficence is common to philosophical discussions of ethics. Beneficence requires that we take positive steps to contribute to our neighbor's health and welfare. By one definition, "it is the duty to help others further their important and legitimate interests when we can do so with minimal risk to ourselves."[11] As such, beneficence is the positive side of "do no harm," which ethicists often call the principle of nonmaleficence. In fact, some ethical theorists combine beneficence and nonmaleficence as two dimensions of the single moral duty of benevolence. This is much like what happens in the catechisms of the Christian churches. When discussing the Ten Commandments, catechisms explain that love not only avoids the behavior the commandment forbids but also seeks the good of the neighbor in like manner.

In popular thinking about ethics, I suspect that most people would identify benevolence with the general feeling that we ought to do good to our neighbor. However, whether we speak of beneficence, as I will, or of benevolence as others do, the point for the moment is that there is a well-established notion that we have a moral obligation to go beyond doing no harm. Furthermore, this is the point at which most would probably see a connection between the ethics of love and the general ethics of the secular world. There is, of course, debate as to whether corporations should be held to the duty of beneficence, as in De George's view earlier in this chapter. That is a question we will engage more fully later. For now, it is sufficient to point out that our previous analysis of business as an order of vocation and anticipation makes it clear, from that theological vantage point, that business has a positive role to play in serving the common good. I will operate with that conviction until we have occasion to examine it again.

If there is, then, considerable popular acceptance of the duty of beneficence and some theological warrants for thinking that economic institutions have such a duty, what does this suggest for the ethics of love in the practice of business? My answer is twofold: (1) Agape differs in significant ways from beneficence but, nonetheless, has a positive relationship to beneficence; and (2) the existence of beneficent behavior and the widespread acceptance of the principle of beneficence help bridge the shareability gap between the Christian love ethic and the ethics of business.

As I have already hinted, the positive outreach of beneficence certainly makes it akin to agape. The previously cited definition of beneficence suggests a point of difference, however. The words "when we can do so with minimal risk to ourselves" place limits and qualifications on how far we are expected to go. Love ultimately knows no limits because it is expressive of the limitless love of God who, in Christ, reveals that no risk is too great for our redemption.

Even if one argues that the caveat about undue risk is not a necessary part of the definition of beneficence and that examples of heroic self-sacrifice are abundant, our customary understanding of the concept is that undue risks are not obligatory. Those who decide against taking a serious risk to help their neighbor are not to be blamed. Consequently, the unconditional character of agape makes it appear to be more of an *ideal* than an ethical principle, and those who fulfill some of its loftiest impulses may even qualify as heroes or saints. Ideals draw us beyond simple duties while including those duties within the framework of their demand.[12] Furthermore, Christian faith insists that the expression of agape in the lives of believers and the community of the church is a product of God's grace at work and not an achievement for which the individual ego can claim credit. This emphasis on God's action in and through our lives gives even the notion of agape as an ideal a special twist that sets it apart.[13]

As an ideal deeply rooted in the experience of divine grace and in the faith life of the Christian community, love can hardly be the prevailing norm of any secular organization, business or otherwise. At the same time, the assumed responsibility corporations have to do good and the compatibility of agape and beneficence, taken together, suggests that love need not be considered alien to the ethos of corporate life. That point, I think, is strengthened as we look further at the positive relation between love and beneficence.

First of all, love affirms beneficence. Persons and communities who aspire to live by love can link arms with those who seek the good of their neighbors and support their efforts. Second, the rich ethical tradition that has grown up around agape can inform and inspire higher levels of beneficence, including guidance in matters of justice and the building of healthy relationships within organizations for, we recall, love embodies equal regard for all and seeks to build community.[14]

With respect to the pluralistic environment of business and society, in which love must coexist with beneficence as well as other ethical concepts, Richard De George has the following to say: "A plurality of moral principles within a society does not necessarily mean irreconcilable diversity. Pluralism on the level of moral principles is compatible with social agreement on the morality of many basic practices. Such agreement does not necessarily involve agreement on the moral principles different people use to evaluate practices."[15] Thus, he continues, we virtually all agree that murder is wrong, but different moral principles, religious and otherwise, may be involved in that common conviction.

This is helpful to our overall purposes, but I think our analysis of agape and beneficence takes us even a step further. While there is a sense in which agape can be the norm of only those who are "in Christ," there is also a sense in which love finds a point of contact in the beneficent impulses of the human spirit. By this observation we are led, then, to the second point mentioned earlier: this "point of contact" offers a bridge across the shareability gap, whereby love becomes intelligible beyond the confines of the faith community. This second point is better illustrated than discussed. Therefore, we proceed to two examples of how the dynamics of agape can find a place in the real world of business ethics. The first example deals with practice and the second with theory.

THE CASE OF PACIFIC BELL: AIDS AND THE EXTRA MILE

In the early years of public awareness of AIDS, Pacific Bell Telephone Company engaged the challenge of AIDS in the workplace with the kind of ethical sensitivity that gained them the praise of the *Wall Street Journal, Newsweek,* and *Business Week.* One expert on the subject cited the case of Pacific Bell as among the role models for the rest of the nation.[16] I think it will be instructive for our present concerns to trace some of the highlights of Pacific Bell's response to AIDS as reported in the *Harvard Business Review,* "Uncommon Decency: Pacific Bell Responds to AIDS."

As the words *uncommon decency* suggest, we have here an instance when the corporation has clearly gone beyond the moral minimum at a time when guidance for corporations in this area of ethical concern was pretty scarce.

When the reality of AIDS became a part of the work scene, Pacific Bell had to face the rampant fear and prejudice that still exist but were especially intense in 1985–86, when there had been less public education and discussion than there are now: "There was a coin collector who refused to touch the phone booths in the predominantly gay Castro district of San Francisco. One Los Angeles crew balked at installing phones in the offices of the L.A. AIDS Foundation and another San Francisco crew insisted on being issued head-to-toe covering before installing phones in General Hospital's AIDS ward. And there was a lineman who refused to use the truck of a fellow employee, rumored to have died of AIDS, until it was sterilized."[17]

Incidents such as those confronted management with the need to deal with their employees' growing anxiety while respecting the rights of employees with AIDS and meeting legitimate public expectations for service. One noteworthy response to this challenge was a union-management agreement to provide a joint AIDS education program to help allay the fears of workers. In addition, union leadership, with management blessing, assembled a list of thirty volunteers, both straight and gay, who were willing to work jobs that other workers felt they could not handle.

Apparently, this strategy was so reassuring that the team was never called upon to step in. In any case, this kind of first response to the crisis struck out for understanding and assurance instead of heading into a union-management conflict.[18]

Pacific Bell's response soon went beyond intervention in a crisis of fear and prejudice to policies and programs designed to meet the needs of persons with AIDS and create a more caring community. First and foremost, the company assured persons with AIDS that they still had jobs. In this they built on a strong tradition of two-way commitment and loyalty between employees and employer. As one manager put it, "We don't fire sick people." Instead, there was a recognition that persons with AIDS needed their work as a reason to go on living.[19]

Persons with AIDS also need their jobs for the essential ongoing medical benefits that go with them. In this regard Pacific Bell's commitment to continue that coverage led to general reforms in its health care policy that benefited not only AIDS patients but persons with other medical problems as well. Less costly and more personal and humane alternatives to hospitalization like hospice care and case-by-case analysis of medical needs were incorporated in the company's approach to providing health care coverage. This kind of initiative, together with the development of company-sponsored support groups for persons with AIDS and regular communications with employees on AIDS issues, helped to create a more sensitive and caring corporate community.[20]

However, the report on Pacific Bell goes on to tell us that the company went beyond the moral minimum not only in the ways described but also in risking leadership in a controversial area of public life. It was one thing to take care of its employees and another to engage in activities that would publicly associate the company with AIDS concerns and, therefore, with "gays, drugs, and contagion." But that is what Pacific Bell did. Pacific Telesis Foundation, established by Pacific Bell's parent company, funded the first AIDS video aimed at business, and Pacific Bell's corporate television group produced it in conjunction with the San Francisco AIDS Foundation. Pacific Bell then went even further into public view on the AIDS agenda by its open opposition to Proposition 64 in the November 1986 election. Had this measure passed, people with the AIDS virus could have been fired from their jobs, students could have been removed from school, and even quarantine could have been enforced. Pacific Bell's contribution to the campaign against the proposition was the largest of any California business. With the video and the political campaign, Pacific Bell went beyond its former cautionary conservatism to assume a new position of leadership.[21]

It is hard to say much about Pacific Bell management's motives or reasons for responding as they did. However, the report on Pacific Bell suggests that a number of different factors were at work. Chuck Woodman, a key manager in the development of the Pacific Bell response, reports how a minister's sermon at the funeral of a worker who had died of AIDS turned him away from a judgmental attitude to one of compassion. Others pushed the company in the direction of concern out of the apparently beneficent conviction that it was morally right. At the same time, more pragmatic considerations of what is politically astute in a center of gay activism like San Francisco were also at work. Moreover, at least one prominent corporate leader at Pacific Bell felt that public advocacy for AIDS concerns would help the company with a pending gay discrimination law suit.[22]

The array of motives and reasons for positive action on AIDS in the workplace that one can safely discern from the report on Pacific Bell is the sort of mix one might expect in any large organization. They run the gamut from the spiritual to the purely practical. However, the point is that moral consensus to go beyond the minimum, to move from self-concern to service, was possible, whatever the diversity of the leadership, and it was possible as a considerable turnaround from past ways of operating. The Pacific Bell case shows that there are points of contact for the ethics of love in the plurality of corporate life. To the extent that Pacific Bell's concern for persons with AIDS showed an ability on the part of a corporation to be self-giving, concerned for the equal dignity of all, and ready to build a community of acceptance and support, there was an atmosphere in which the spirit of love could breathe freely.

A COVENANTAL MODEL FOR BUSINESS ETHICS

In her book *Good Intentions Aside: A Manager's Guide to Resolving Ethical Problems,* business ethicist Laura Nash offers what she calls "a covenantal business ethic" as an alternative to the traditional, bottom-line oriented, enlightened self-interest approach to business problem solving. The details of her covenantal theory are spelled out in her account of what she considers to be the three conditions of ethical problem solving in business.

Condition number one is "integrating ethical norms with the pursuit of economic success." The idea here is to make one's ethical commitments an integral part of the total decision-making process of the corporation so that management is not caught in the bind of having to choose *either* what is ethical *or* what is profitable; the two must go hand in hand. The key to making this happen is in taking a covenantal outlook. In the covenantal outlook, business problem solving becomes inherently ethical because business understands itself to be involved in a covenantal relationship with its stakeholders. In this relationship the purpose of business is to create and deliver value to meet other people's needs. For this delivered value it receives a return, which it naturally needs to prosper. However, its focus is on delivering created value, and its driving assumption is that it should be creating mutually enabling relationships through service to others. When one understands the purpose and makeup of the company as enabling a mutually beneficial set of relationships for all stakeholders, one's approach to problem solving shifts from strict bottom-line calculations to more humane patterns of thinking.[23]

Condition number two, "an other-directed attitude," follows logically from the first. A covenantal ethic requires an attitude or character in which other people's needs become the *first* purpose of business. Nash wants to call managers to a higher level of moral development than self-interest. She advocates an other-directedness in which genuine caring for others replaces self-interest. Caring, in turn, animates service that is geared to the needs and terms of those served. An outlook of self-interest can, of course, be attentive to the needs and wants of others and the quality of the service given, but it will do so for its own interests in profit. A truly caring, other-directed attitude will finally distinguish itself in the quality of concern and service given.[24] The differences between self-interest and other-directedness are "much like the differences between manipulation and love. Do you try to meet your spouse's needs primarily because it is in your interest to do so, or do you service them because you care? Which marriage is likelier to prosper and be a mutually beneficial relationship: the one based on self-interest or the one based on genuine caring?"[25]

Nash's final condition, "a business ethics must be capable of motivating pragmatic and competitive behavior," focuses on the kind of relational thinking that is correlated with the ethics of service. The more service-oriented our company ethos is, the more relationship-oriented our thinking (and, we may presume, vice versa). If you are operating in terms of the service-relationship correlation, there is a built-in motivational dynamic: "If you are relationship-oriented, you automatically measure and motivate yourself with reference to the state of affairs between you and the other person, be it customer, employee, shareholder, supplier, distributor, or the public."[26] The maintenance of strong, value-laden, and trusting relationships in a service-oriented business attitude is not only an ethically responsible posture from the covenantal standpoint but it is pragmatic and competitive as well. Quality of service, many believe, is the competitive edge of the future, and well-established, trusting, and mutually beneficial relationships with stakeholders may be the best predictor of future success.[27]

Although she is well aware that she is advocating an ethical mind-set that stands in contrast to dominant trends in the tradition of business, Nash is also able to demonstrate the reality and success of covenant thinking in the actual practice of contemporary business. Her theoretical points are punctuated with examples of managers and corporations who have dealt with ethical challenges from a de facto covenant perspective and come out ahead for having done so.

Everyone writing in the field of business ethics, it sometimes seems, uses the example of Johnson & Johnson's ethically admirable response to the Tylenol crisis. Nash is no exception, but she also gives us an incident from the history of the same company that is even more interesting in some respects because it demonstrates ethical behavior when the public was not looking.

After years of successfully marketing its profitable baby oil as a tanning agent, management was faced with the need to reevaluate whether such marketing was still ethical. Early and not yet widely circulated or generally confirmed evidence surfaced that tanning may not be healthy. Johnson & Johnson could have kept on with the same marketing pitch until the scientific evidence and the political atmosphere became clearer. This, says Nash, is the likely response of a self-interested approach to problem solving. But Johnson & Johnson responded by immediately dropping their claims for baby oil as a tanning agent and absorbed a 50 percent drop in sales during the first year of that decision. They then rebounded by developing other ways in which the product could serve people's needs. Such a decision was integral to their corporate thinking, it was other-directed in concern for customer health, and it inspired new competitive initiatives for service. It is a good example of the three conditions of covenantal thinking in ethics.[28]

As we review Nash's covenantal business ethic, we can already see some clear connections with the ethics of love. Indeed, she herself notes that her comments on the concepts of covenant and service have deep roots in the Jewish and Christian traditions of biblical ethics. That connection is underscored when we take a brief look at the covenantal model of Christian ethics developed by Joseph L. Allen on the basis of biblical ideas of covenant.

Allen identifies the six characteristics of God's covenant love: "God (1) binds us together as members of a covenant community, (2) affirms the worth of each covenant member, (3) extends covenant love inclusively, (4) seeks to meet the needs of each member of the covenant community, (5) is steadfast, and (6) is reconciling."[29] This covenant love extends to all people, uniting us all in a universal covenant with God and each other in which our covenant love for one another is to reflect the same characteristics as God's covenant love. This all-inclusive covenant is both God's original intention in creation and God's promise for the future fulfillment of the divine dominion.[30]

Parenthetically, we should note that Allen's account of love is much like that we have already sketched. It is rooted in an understanding of the will and promise of God and fueled by the experience of being loved. The six characteristics of covenant love clearly correspond to the all-inclusive and reconciling or community-building character of love that we discerned.

Although we are called to love as we have first been loved in all our relationships (the implication of the universal covenant), we are also called to care for each other in a variety of *special covenants*. Special covenants include various sets of relationships of trust that people have entered into for some specific purpose. These relationships include family, government, economic institutions like corporations, and associations. The idea of special covenants is akin to the idea of orders of vocation set forth in chapter 4.[31]

The ethical obligations we have in special covenants differ in some respects from the obligation of covenant love that we have for all people in the inclusive, universal covenant God has established. In special covenants there are limits on our obligation imposed by the agreements that shape the organization, the restrictions of its membership, and the distinct purposes for which it exists. Nonetheless, special covenants still involve the kind of covenant love that is the keystone of biblical ethics. In both the inclusive covenant we have with all people and the special covenants in which we participate, respect for the worth of all, concern for the needs of all, and the kind of faithfulness that cements and builds relationships of trust are all required.[32]

We need not belabor the comparison between Nash's covenantal business ethic and Allen's covenant love model to conclude that there is a high degree of shareability between the two. The fact that Nash demonstrates that the seeds of her ideas are there in the performance of noteworthy businesses and managers makes her proposal all the more promising as a point of contact for Christian witness in the ethics of business.

I also think Nash's understanding of covenantal business ethics makes an important contribution to the issue of motive. Instead of simply saying that good ethics is good for business, as one often hears, Nash advocates integrating concern for ethics with concern for economic success and making the impulse of service to others the spur for innovative and competitive business initiatives. In her account, then, a business is not ethical in order to succeed but tries to succeed in the service of its ethical commitments and governs its efforts at success according to those commitments.

In the ethics of self-giving Christian love, the status of self-love is much like the status of profitability in the Nash system. Attention to the self's interests, when integrated with a deep commitment to agape or covenant love, affirms others in affirming the self and cares for the self so that it is able to serve others.[33] If one is to be self-giving in love, one must have a self to give. If a corporation or a business is to produce shared value and meet human needs, it must be economically successful.

In the next four chapters we continue to conduct our dialogue between the Christian ethics of love and the issues of ethics in business. Our quest is for points of contact on which to conduct the dialogue and to see how the Christian ethic can take us *beyond* the ethics of conventional morality in insight, spirit, and practice.

6

BEYOND LEADERSHIP TO
SERVANT LEADERSHIP

A recently retired top executive at a nationally known company spoke eloquently of how the ethos of the company's founder pervaded the life of the corporation. His strong principles and Christian values had assured that the company would be "a high-minded organization." No one who worked there could escape being exposed to that tradition; they were expected to live by it.

Now, my friend told me, things are very different. The corporation has been bought by a larger, highly diversified corporation and become a division of that organization. Not only does the new management not have a feel for the product line and the industry itself but also they do not have a feel for the values of the original founder. The memory and influence of that industry giant are fading fast.

This has become an oft-told story in recent times. The National Institute for Business Management has cited constantly changing company ownership as a significant factor in the erosion of ethical standards in businesses since the heyday of corporate raiding and company buyouts in the 1980s. Turnover hampers the developing and sustaining of ethical standards in several ways. First of all, as in my opening example, it dilutes the corporate culture and ethos. Second, the game of buying and selling companies tends to focus on short-term profits at the expense of long-range concerns for the quality of the business. Finally, it undermines employee loyalty. When a relationship of mutual commitment and trust does not exist between employees and owners, the conditions are not favorable for the development of a strong ethical tradition.[1]

THE IMPORTANCE OF CHARACTER

Situations and incidents such as these raise the issue of the ethical significance of character in business leadership and the character of the corporate culture it shapes and by which it is shaped. The quality of ethical leadership in business and the ethical quality of the corporate culture are not only major items on the current business ethics agenda, as we have seen, but also they have their counterparts in the general discussion of ethics. Ethicists, both philosophers and theologians, have become increasingly interested in the subject of character and the manner in which the character of the communities in which we live shape our characters individually.

For a long time ethics has concentrated on the formulation of principles of right and wrong and their application to specific ethical problems. This will continue to be the important work of ethical reflection and practice. However, some are saying that our preoccupation with ethical problem solving has resulted in a neglect of concern for "character," the sorts of people we are. These newer voices are suggesting that our moral development, our ethical formation, and the shaping of our conscience are even more important than formulating the rules of right and wrong and applying them. Persons of integrity and communities with strong, clear ethical traditions possess the "character" needed to do the right thing. An overemphasis on decision making puts the cart before the horse.[2]

In the preface to his book *Managing with Integrity,* management professor Charles E. Watson observes that in ethics in general and business ethics in particular, people gravitate toward codes or rational analysis of ethical problems as their chosen ways to change or motivate moral behavior. However, as important as both these approaches are, our ethical behavior is really shaped by our vision of the good and the way in which it claims our hearts. He is speaking of the foundations of character, and, in his judgment, ethical inquiry should begin with character: "By focusing on character and its development, it is possible to reach beyond the sterile domain and limited focus [codes and rational analysis] heretofore taken by ethics."[3]

Parenthetically, Watson also notes that, in the consideration of character development, religious influences should not be disdained. "To cast aside, arbitrarily, what has obviously been a major part of the human experience and a significant influence on the course of civilization [i.e., religion] is limiting."[4]

Character is shaped in community where community has formed around a "story" that binds people together. The leaders of the community are those who keep the story alive. The moral vision or character of the world Jewish community is shaped by the biblical story of the chosen people, centuries of exile, and their struggle to regain and retain the promised land. African Americans are formed in their character and conscience by their story of slavery, oppression, and the struggle for freedom. Leaders like Malcolm X and Martin Luther King Jr. have kept the story alive and drawn out its ethical implications. Even professions have communities whose character is shaped by a particular story. The medical profession has a character or professional conscience deeply embedded in the traditions of healing and in the sacred covenant between physician and patient.[5]

Being part of a community and the story by which it lives has a significant impact on the sorts of people we are. Thus, as noted in the last chapter, to be part of the Christian community and the story of Jesus is to be formed in love, to have a character imbued with the experience of God's love in Christ and all the ethical implications that follow.

Business organizations are also potentially communities with stories, stories that shape the corporate culture or character with leaders who keep the story alive. So, in the conversation I reported, my friend recalled how the company founder developed a company story of quality and integrity that was kept alive by other leaders who were affected by that story. A distinctive ethical vision was perpetuated until a new regime came in.

Character, the ethical constitution and orientation of business leaders and corporate cultures, provides the essential foundations for high ethical standards and practices in business. It is a key point of dialogue for the work of faith in the ethics of business.

BUSINESS LEADERSHIP AND CHRISTIAN SERVANTHOOD

At first glance, a marriage of business leadership philosophy and the virtues of Christian servanthood would seem doomed to fall apart on the basis of "irreconcilable differences." However, when we get beyond the stereotypes of each of them, we discover some real avenues of compatibility. It is possible to blend the values of both traditions. On the basis of what he has written and the testimony of those who know him, no one makes this clearer than Max De Pree, CEO of Herman Miller, the Michigan based furniture company. Herman Miller is a Fortune 500 company that ranked seventh in the nation during the 1980s in total return to investors and, in a 1988 *Fortune* poll, was picked among the ten most admired companies, ranking first in its industry and fourth overall for quality of products and services.[6]

As I write this chapter, De Pree's *Leadership Is an Art* has been one of the hottest leadership books for the past couple years.[7] De Pree's thought and example have also had a profound influence on the development of Laura Nash's business ethic, which we just reviewed.[8] Themes of covenant and service, so prominent in Nash's theory, emerge clearly in De Pree's leadership philosophy as a direct expression of his Christian faith and his upbringing in the Calvinist tradition. Although he speaks very clearly as a successful business leader, he does not hesitate to infuse his thought with the resources of his faith. But he does so in ways that are constructive and respectful of the diverse members of his company. Through his leadership, elements of the Christian story contribute to the ongoing development of the Herman Miller story. Max De Pree's definition of the art of leadership is "liberating people to do what is required of them in the most effective and humane way."[9] There is a great deal of ethical significance packed into this brief statement. First and foremost, the statement says that, in the workplace (for De Pree this is just as appropriate a venue for realizing the values of self-fulfillment as private life), good leadership enables people to be the best of what they are, to realize their fullest potential. This recognizes the innate dignity and worth of each individual, and it affirms the diversity of gifts and experience possessed by the variety of people that make up an organization.[10]

Actively promoting the dignity of all and celebrating our diversity as a human community are virtues of leadership that echo the character of Christian love in what we have seen is its inclusive embrace of all people. It evokes memories of Joseph Allen's discussion of the universal, inclusive covenant of God's love that becomes the model for our love. De Pree himself helps us make these theological connections: "as a Christian I believe each person is made in the image of God. For those of us who have received the gift of leadership from the people we lead, this belief has enormous implications."[11]

Among the implications of this conviction, I believe, are those rights that De Pree thinks are essential for the fulfillment of life at work. Among these eight rights is the right to be needed. This means that each of us has the opportunity to use our best gifts to the maximum in concert with the goals and needs of the company. Closely related to it is the right to be involved, to have one's input valued, and to have regular means by which to make a contribution to the company decision making. People also have a right to understand and a right to affect their own destiny. We need to know where we stand, what the company direction is, and how we fit in. We need to be clear about expectations, criteria of performance, and promises made to us. And we need the opportunity to participate in our evaluations and the decisions made about our career futures.[12]

I could not help but remember some of these "rights" during a recent conversation with a manager at a regional phone company. He complained of how he was about to take on another job, his third managerial move without an increase in pay or rating. The problem, as he sees it, is that his performance evaluations are good; therefore, his superiors move him laterally to wherever they have troubles. This is helping them earn good marks, but it is not helping him get ahead in his career development. Moreover, the worst part, in his mind, was that he was not consulted.

This phone company manager has been deprived of several of the rights already mentioned. He is also in need of being granted De Pree's final right, the right to make a commitment: "To make a commitment, any employee should be able to answer 'yes' to the following question: Is this a place where they will let me do my best? How can leaders expect a commitment from the people they lead, if those people are thwarted and hindered?"[13] For the time being, at least, this particular employee's commitment to work is rooted in the fact that he has four teenagers to feed who are on their way to college.

The leadership that frees people to be their best, that affirms them in their diversity, and that includes them in the dreams, decisions, and benefits of the organization is a servant leadership. This is how Max De Pree sees it. Unlike the phone company manager's bosses, who sacrificed his advancement for their own benefit, servant leadership is ready to take the risks and make the sacrifices needed for employees to have real opportunities and genuine participation.[14]

Recent debates over the ethics of high executive compensation suggest that there is likely a real need for the kind of servant character that can provide leadership in this area. The issue of executive pay was aired in an article in the journal *Business Ethics* during the fall of 1991. The article points out that executives and CEOs have been receiving enormous pay increases that have created a huge gap between their salaries and the salary of the average employee in their firms: "In 1990, according to *Business Week*, CEOs at major American corporations made eighty-five times the pay of the average factory worker. In Japan, by contrast, the average CEO makes seventeen times what the average worker makes. What's more, CEO pay in the U.S. has risen 212 percent in the last decade, while worker pay has risen only 54 percent."[15] According to *Fortune*, such disparities create a trust gap that threatens to undermine morale.[16]

The matter of morale becomes even more serious, one presumes, when large pay packages are awarded to top executives at a time when their companies are turning in lackluster performances and laying off workers. To make matters worse, some students of the problem, like Graef Crystal, who wrote *In Search of Excess*, a respected study of executive compensation, see evidence of collusion in the awarding of inordinately high salaries. The directors, who recruit top executives and set salaries, together with the compensation specialists and search firms who help them, all have a stake in the CEO's having a high salary. For the professionals, it means their percentage is worth more if the executive's package is larger.

The directors, "because they're members of the same privileged caste, view CEOS as somehow laden with special talents worthy of great rewards."[17]

There are legislative and stockholder initiatives that can be taken to alleviate the problem. However, above all, some servant leadership on the part of top executives of major companies will be needed. Otherwise, the pattern will tend to perpetuate itself because placing a cap on executive salaries may make it hard to recruit the best people, a risk boards will not want to take.

Not surprisingly, Max De Pree is featured in this report as one who has exerted the sort of leadership needed, but there are others, including Chuck Denny, CEO of ADC Telecommunications. In Denny's mind, when executive compensation is overdone, it is a violation of the corporate covenant relationship in which people live and work: "There is implicit in any organization a social contract that exists between those who work and those who manage. It is part of the culture, part of the myth. People have to make judgments as to whether there is a just sharing of the fruits of the enterprise, particularly when those fruits become severely limited."[18]

Denny's words suggest to us that a servant-oriented character attuned to the needs of others is a character oriented to justice. Justice in its simplest terms, going back to Aristotle's definition, is that each should receive his or her due.

Whether in matters of fair compensation or other management practices that maximize the opportunities and benefits of employees and respect their contributions, the kind of servant leadership De Pree and others advocate resonates well with the New Testament ideal of servanthood or service, which is an expression of the character of love.

Against the backdrop of the Greek cultural traditions, which formed the milieu of the New Testament church, Jesus' teachings on service (the Greek word is *diakonia*) are revolutionary. For the Greeks, ruling was the truly fulfilling position to which one should aspire, not serving. Serving was considered undesirable and undignified. The service of the statesman to the state was honorable, but it was still thought of as self-fulfilling rather than an exercise in self-giving.[19] For Jesus, service and servanthood are the marks of true discipleship and the traits that characterize his own person and work. Jesus' comments in Matthew 20:25-28 bring the contrast into sharp focus: "'You know that the rulers of the Gentiles lord it over them, and their great ones are tyrants over them. It will not be so among you; but whoever wishes to be great among you must be your servant, and whoever wishes to be first among you must be your slave; just as the Son of Man came not to be served but to serve, and to give his life as a ransom for many.'"

This is a strong theme throughout the New Testament account of discipleship and the life of love. We have already looked at Paul's admonition in Philippians 2 that we should have the mind of Christ, who emptied himself and took the form of a servant. We have the example of Jesus washing the feet of the disciples. In Luke 22:27, Jesus compares himself to one who serves at table rather than one who sits and is served. Through the eyes of faith, the Christian community sees Jesus as the fulfillment of Isaiah's prophetic account of the Suffering Servant who has borne our sufferings and suffered for our sins (Isaiah 53).

Obviously, the biblical discussion of *diakonia* in its various forms will not provide a detailed blueprint for servant leadership in business. However, it is vital to the character of a leadership that is dedicated to the rights and needs of those entrusted to it. And there is a strong sense of servant leadership among many executives. Some of this is rooted in Christian formation, as we have seen it is in De Pree's case. Another example of faith-based thinking about the character of leadership is evident in a published interview with Thomas S. Johnson. A faithful Catholic and former president of Manufacturers Hanover Trust and Chemical Bank, Johnson professes an other-centered brand of leadership that typifies the servant leader:

> I try to lead in a way that brings out the best in others. If work is to be fulfilling, it must be conducted in a setting that is respectful of human needs and moral values. The large organizations in which we work must be designed not merely according to theoretical engineering or economic formulations, but in a way that adequately considers the impact that work in these organizations has on the individuals there.[20]

Not all who sense the need for service in leadership style are rooted in religious convictions, however. Charles E. Watson interviewed 125 CEOs and senior executives. His findings turned up a high instance of the basic conviction that we are not here just to serve our own desires but primarily or, at least, additionally the needs of others. Again, not all of the people responding in that way did so from faith, as I have suggested, but Watson's summary of their combined input almost paraphrases Jesus: "The point is this: life takes on meaning only as it is spent. Only through service do people achieve greatness."[21]

INSTRUMENTAL VALUE AND LEADERSHIP SKILLS

In the wake of the 1992 Democratic convention, columnist Mike Royko, with his typical sarcasm, told a story that raises a social problem not addressed by the Democratic platform. The story is about Bob, who fathers children and runs away; Eileen, who gets pregnant by Bob; and a bureaucracy, whose mishandling of Bob's child support payments ends up costing the taxpayers thousands of dollars. Royko proceeds to ask whether the Democratic platform says anything about the evident stupidity in the behavior displayed by all concerned: Bob is irresponsible, Eileen is gullible, and the bureaucrats are bumbling. The question is rhetorical, of course. Royko concludes that one of our great social problems,"galloping individual stupidity," is not covered in the party platform.[22]

Royko's comments are tongue in cheek, but they do suggest a point for us to note. Any system—political, bureaucratic, or ethical—is no better than the people involved. Leadership in the building of an ethical organization requires character and, also, the skills to implement the ethical vision in an effective way.

Although Max De Pree's discussions of leadership and corporate culture are infused with substantive ethical significance—for him, leadership is identical with ethical leadership—much of the burgeoning literature on leadership focuses primarily on skills. However, skills for effective leadership have an important role to play in the service of ethical goals. Skills, like organizational procedures and policies, are the means to an end. They have what ethicists sometimes call an instrumental value. They help us promote and achieve those values of human well-being that are properly ends in themselves and the targets of moral obligation. Much of the work of ethics in business is to develop strategies, skills, and organizational structures that work in business and facilitate the morally significant values we seek to attain. This is a major reason why so many who teach and consult in business ethics advocate the integration of ethical concerns and commitments with the general structure of corporate policy and decision making.

A sampling from one of the better volumes on leadership should be sufficient to illustrate my point. *Leaders* by Warren Bennis and Burt Nanus sets forth a philosophy and strategies of effective leadership based on the study of leadership skills among a variety of leaders from all walks of life. The statement at the heart of their proposal is "Managers are people who do things right and leaders are people who do the right thing."[23] The distinction is between *efficiency* and *effectiveness,* the mastery of routines or the nuts-and-bolts daily operations versus the ability to move things forward. To be such a leader, to be effective, a person who does the right thing, is directly related to one of the four keys of effective leadership the authors identify: being vision-oriented.[24]

The leader works with the emotional and spiritual resources of the organization, which are the stuff of its vision and the leader's vision. The manager works with the physical resources of the organization, such as capital, personnel skills, raw materials, and technology, to ensure security, productivity, and quality. That is important work. However, it is the effective leader who can provide the vision that builds pride and satisfaction and inspires workers to higher levels of achievement by showing them the meaning and the value of their work. The leader attends to "the most fundamental of human needs—the need to be important, to make a difference, to feel useful, to be a part of a successful and worthwhile enterprise."[25]

Clearly, the content of the vision needs to be filled in, but the nurturing of a vision that is responsive to the needs of the human spirit is a leadership skill and an organizational goal commensurate with the infusion of ethical sensitivities in the ethos of management and the culture of the corporation.

In a similar fashion, the development of self-regard, a component of yet another of the four keys, is an exercise that has a potential payoff for sound leadership ethics as well as effectiveness. The authors point out that those who have high self-esteem are less likely to rely on negative criticism to motivate employees and more likely to operate on a solid foundation of affirmation, upon which they can build motivation and constructive criticism.[26] Here again, we have an approach friendly to ethical concerns for respect for persons and for enabling them to be their best. It's probably pushing things a bit, but there seem to be echoes here of "love your neighbor as yourself" and the corollary understanding that God claims us and moves us by loving us and forgiving us, not by condemning us.

There are many other skills of leadership, like understanding how the organization runs its "social architecture" (e.g., collegial versus hierarchical) so that you can make it work for desired values or change it to serve those values better.[27] Skills like these are necessary if ethical ideals are to be incorporated in the mainstream of organizational life. Similarly, leadership skills in building trust, another part of one of the authors' keys, are clearly a servant to building the kinds of relationships that are enriching and can even be covenantal in character.[28]

Although leadership skill and organizational strategies have instrumental value for the cause of integrating ethics and moral character in leadership and the organization's culture, they can also be counterproductive to achieving the values we are morally obligated to seek for the well-being of all. Leadership skills and organizational strategies can be coercive or manipulative. Thus, while the appearance of effectively meeting ethical goals may be present in a given case, the ownership of these principles and values may not run very deep among employees. Ethics without ownership is not ethics; it is merely compliance.

In other cases, certain kinds of effective leadership can be built on models inappropriate to ethical goals. Thus, corporate leadership may commit itself to lofty ethical principles but not make the revisions in company structure needed for subordinates to act on those principles. If corporate structure has proven effective in other respects such as productivity, profitability, and employee satisfaction, it may be hard to see that it is out of synch with ethical goals. A strict "chain of command" structure, for example, in which everyone has one boss and one boss only, can be a very efficient form of management, but it can also stifle the kind of open, broad-based communication and sharing in the corporate community that is necessary to integrating ethics and the operation.[29]

Means and ends are interrelated. Evaluating the compatibility of means and ends is an important part of ethics. Christian ethics may have little to say about the sciences of leadership theory and organizational theory. However, it does have a contribution to make in asking whether various options maximize freedom of conscience, enable people to make ethically responsible decisions, and encourage the formation of a community of moral consensus rather than simply a community of conformity.

One of the good things about the leadership theory elaborated by Bennis and Nanus is that it is geared to all levels of the organization, from the shop floor to the executive suite. This enhances the possibility that conscientious, ethical leadership will pervade the entire organization.

At the same time, not every effort to stress broad participation in leadership has the desired effect. Despite the positive potential of the "total quality management" movement, which operates with extensive employee involvement in decision making, the way it is implemented is crucial. It can easily become a burden for confused middle managers and fearful employees as they struggle to reorient themselves to a different configuration of power in reaching decisions.[30]

CHARACTER AND CORPORATE CULTURE

One hears a great deal about corporate culture and how it is a key to an ethical company. As with the leadership that shapes it and is shaped by it, corporate culture, ethically speaking, is a matter of character. Communities, like individuals, have character, as we have noted.

In Max De Pree's discussion of leadership, he moves freely between ideas on leadership and ideas on corporate culture or corporate values. There is no question in his mind that there needs to be a culture of values that mold the company community: "Shared ideals, shared ideas, shared goals, shared respect, a sense of integrity, a sense of quality, a sense of caring—these are the basis of Herman Miller's covenant and values system."[31] And there need to be "tribal storytellers" to keep this shared story alive.[32]

For De Pree the Herman Miller "story" or culture is one built on the notion of inclusive covenantal relationships in which the dignity of all and the affirmation of the diversity of people in the corporate community is grounded in the biblical teaching that we are all created in God's image. What it means is that people and relationships are more important than contracts and corporate structures. The latter are important, but they exist to serve the former.[33] Laura Nash has been inspired to work this out in theory by the way De Pree has worked it out in practice.

Again, lest we think that a theologically alert Max De Pree is unique in building an ethically sensitive corporation, it is well to look at another example.

In a 1990 interview with CEO Robert D. Haas, *Harvard Business Review* gives us a glimpse of the corporate culture and character of Levi Strauss, the much-admired manufacturer of jeans and, now, Dockers. The Levi Strauss leadership has been a part of the Haas family heritage for generations. Robert Haas is building on a long story of ethically responsible management and ethically progressive vision. What we see in our glimpse of this company is the embodiment of certain ethical principles fostered by organizational and leadership strategies of "empowerment" that go forward under the banner of the "aspirations statement."[34]

Certain ethical values and principles that emerge in the profile of Levi Strauss and its leadership give us a snapshot of the character of its corporate culture. First of all, although Levi Strauss has a tradition of "paternalism" in the sense of taking care of its people, it does not practice paternalism in the sense of controlling people. Rather, the company has taken steps to foster *autonomy* by respecting its employees and giving them the chance to take responsibility into their own hands. To honor the value of autonomy is to enable people to be their best. In terms of biblical anthropology, it means to affirm persons' dignity by giving them the freedom and opportunity to be responsible, rather than manipulating or dominating them, for freedom and responsibility are the core of our personhood as creatures made in God's image. In terms of the ethics of love, respect for autonomy is a facet of love's commitment to enable people to be what they are meant to be to the fullest extent possible: healthy, whole, alive, *free, and responsible.*[35]

At Levi Strauss the imperative associated with the value of autonomy is *empowerment*. The aspirations statement defines it this way: "Leadership that increases the authority and responsibility of those closest to our products and customers. By actively pushing responsibility, trust, and recognition into the organization, we can harness and release the capabilities of all our people."[36] The old paternalism in which people were dependent and passively did what they were told has been eclipsed.

Equality and dignity are certainly served by respect for autonomy that extends throughout the corporate community. Equality and dignity are also served by the affirmation of diversity. The aspirations statement explicitly affirms diversity of, for example, age, sex, and ethnicity at all levels of the organization. Moreover, this diversity is viewed as a rich resource rather than something to be suppressed or brought into conformity with uniform ways of thinking. "Differing points of view will be sought; diversity will be valued and honesty rewarded, not suppressed."[37] Needless to say, this kind of openness is not only essential to justice in a pluralistic world but also congenial to the kind of dialogue I have advocated in the earlier chapters, the kind of dialogue that can help bridge the shareability gap.

To value and be open to a variety of viewpoints in the midst of diversity is to be a friend of truthfulness. Such openness means that finding the truth in and through the diverse contributions of diverse people is more important than doggedly holding on to cherished thoughts and opinions. Openness to the truth builds community and relationships out of diversity. Refusing to entertain the contributions of others leads to coercion and division.

Robert Haas comments that doing things "my way" and no other way may have worked well in a hierarchical structure but not under empowerment, where diversity is valued. The quest for truth in diversity even means a management that can be truthful about itself, admitting its own vulnerabilities and failures.[38]

When employees are respected, given responsibility, allowed to be themselves rather than controlled, even allowed to disagree, to be empowered instead of overpowered, then we begin to see a picture of covenantal relationships coming into focus that looks much like the portrait painted by De Pree. Although there is still such a thing as management and different degrees of authority, relations are governed by the ethics of concern for persons instead of sheer exercise of power. Thus, employees can challenge their supervisors and argue for a different decision on the basis of values in the aspirations statement, and matters of company policy, such as ways to balance work and family responsibilities, are dealt with collegially.[39]

CONSCIENCE OR CALCULATION

Principles and skills of leadership and features of corporate culture in organizations like Levi Strauss embody a character and provide vehicles for principles and values that Christians can readily affirm, even though the origin of these things may not be in explicitly Christian sources. However, we frequently hear business leaders talk about the character of good leadership and the ethical dimensions of corporate culture in its concern for empowerment, diversity, social responsibility, and the like as things that are not simply ethical but also important to business success and effective in promoting employee loyalty, morale, and productivity. This begins to sound like a mixed signal: an appeal to ethical convictions blended with a testimony to the effect that being good and doing right is good for business. In other words, justice is not its own reward after all. It is reminiscent of those stewardship testimonials we often hear in church in which people who tithe remark that the more they give, the more they are blessed by God with material wealth.

It is, of course, possible to say that good ethics are compatible with good business, as long as we are clear that authentic moral motivation is based on convictions, not calculations about what will pay off in the long run. In fact, a strong ethical tradition in leadership and corporate culture usually is compatible with success, but not necessarily so. One business-man with whom I spoke insisted in the strongest possible terms that we should not connect ethics to success in business. From his Christian per-spective, we should commit ourselves to ethical standards because they are right and we care about our neighbors, not because they are prof-itable in some sense.

If ethical principles and values are not grounded in more than business calculations, they may be endangered. Ethically responsible practices that are generous to employees, customers, stockholders, the society, and the environment can easily be threatened if conditions in the market-place do not favor a consistent application of these policies. One of my conversation partners at the beginning of this study, a corporate veteran who had been CEO of three different organizations, advised me to study the ethics of companies during times of prosperity and compare them with their ethical performance at times of recession. He felt that some noteworthy differences would emerge.

If we are to advocate a corporate culture in which ethics inform prac-tice rather than one in which expediency outranks ethics, then we must raise the issue of whether corporations have consciences to begin with. Do such organizations really have "character" in the sense of a genuine moral viewpoint and the responsibility to act out of that viewpoint, as I have been saying? Once again, we meet the issue of the moral status of corpo-rations and what is justifiable to expect of them in the realm of ethics.

Kenneth E. Goodpaster and John B. Matthews Jr. have taken on those who reject the idea that corporations can have a conscience. They begin their discussion with the case study of a southern steel company during the civil rights activities of the 1960s. The company had made great strides in equal employment and charitable support of black housing, education, and businesses. However, it refused to use its economic power to create further change in local banks, suppliers, and government. The CEO at that time justified his decision by saying that corporations are not "persons" and do not have the same moral obligations to take action and become a change agent in society. Corporations are creations of economic forces and political sanctions and should not be expected to go beyond the moral minimum.[40]

To punctuate the CEO's position, the authors quote philosopher John Ladd, who takes the position a step further in asserting that formal organizations and their official representatives cannot be associated with moral virtues and actions or expected to possess moral integrity. The logic of morality does not fit the logic of organizational life.[41] Although somewhat more nuanced, perhaps, than Ladd's position or that of the steel company CEO, we have seen in the last chapter that Richard De George holds a similar view, even though he stresses that business should not be considered amoral.

Those who are uneasy with the idea of a corporate conscience frequently argue that ethical constraints on corporate behavior appropriately arise from the "invisible hand" of market workings or the regulations of government. In both cases, corporations should stick to the pursuit of economic goals. The view that an organization should develop an independent ethical vision that is integral to decision making and a responsibility of managerial leadership would surely be rejected.[42]

Goodpaster and Matthews advance the contrary opinion that corporations can and ought to have consciences. First of all, their decision making in morally significant matters has the characteristics of ethical reasoning and respect for the needs and rights of others that we associate with the ethical behavior of persons. Furthermore, a business as an organic unity interacting with stakeholders, society, and the environment is as open to ethical demands as a person and is as adaptable to meeting them as it is to providing economic service. Finally, neither government regulation nor market forces are capable of providing adequate moral guidance for corporations any more than the law can cover all the ground of moral obligation for individuals.[43]

The authors go on to respond to the objections they anticipate would be lodged against their stance. We lack space to summarize this entire discussion, but their reply to the objection that corporations are not persons is worth quoting:

> Our frame of reference does not imply that corporations are persons in the literal sense. It simply means that in certain respects concepts and functions normally attributed to persons can also be attributed to organizations made up of persons. Goals, economic values, strategies, and other such

personal attributes are often usefully projected to the corporate level by managers and researchers. Why should we not project the functions of conscience in the same way? As for holding corporations responsible, recent criminal prosecutions such as the case of Ford Motor Company and its Pinto gas tanks suggest that society finds the idea both intelligible and useful.[44]

The case for a corporate conscience fits nicely with the emphasis on the ethics of "character" in the formation of leadership and corporate culture. It also fits into the larger scheme of our theological understanding of economic institutions as orders of vocation and anticipation, which I set forth in chapter 4.

In organizations where character and conscience are in short supply, Christians have an obvious role to play in promoting a new consciousness. In organizations where the traditions of leadership and corporate culture display a strong ethical character and give evidence of a conscience, Christians will find themselves supporting and affirming many of the policies and decisions that result. They may not even have much to add by way of new ethical insight on specific issues of corporate life. However, what they may be able to do best is continually to help their colleagues remain clear on the fact that ethics are not just a luxury one can afford in prosperity or something "added," the primary value of which is that it is good for business. Rather, ethics represent those precious values of the common good that business finally exists to serve.

7

BEYOND
AFFIRMATIVE ACTION

The first phase of the 1992 presidential campaign battle between President George Bush and Governor Bill Clinton was characterized by a struggle to capture the high ground of so-called family values. This amorphous idea seemed to refer to the recovery of traditional values associated with an assumed consensus on what is best in the American way of life. The way in which this appeal was nuanced in addressing specific matters such as abortion, gay rights, affirmative action, welfare, or the plight of the middle class differed, of course, according to who was speaking. In the minds of some observers, however, no matter who was doing the talking, the appeals to "values" were veiled efforts to capture the white middle-class vote.[1]

Whether the analysts were correct in their interpretation of certain forms of campaign rhetoric, one suspects they were at least basing their hunches on the reality of a resurgent prejudice exacerbated by a faltering economy. Tough times tend to bring to the surface incipient racist, classist, and sexist attitudes as people lash out at affirmative action programs, welfare programs, and other policies they perceive to be a threat to their own security and opportunity. At times like that, we are reminded of the need for vigilance in monitoring and confronting the "isms" that foster injustice.

Issues of discrimination in the workplace, then, continue to command our attention. From the standpoint of Christian ethics, we have an opportunity to express the church's broader social witness through participation in the dialogue on these justice concerns in the business universe. In so doing, Christians exercise the witnessing function of ethics as an integral part of their vocation. At the end of chapter 2, I spoke of that witness as an expression of hope and anticipation. In line with that, I reiterate: When Christians seek justice, equality, and dignity for all people, they anticipate the fulfillment of these values in the fullness of God's future reign. They act out a hope rooted in the promise of Jesus for that reign.

In the Christian witness of anticipation, as illustrated in the battle against discrimination and for equality, the ethics of moving from self to service are complemented by our witness to the gospel promise of God's reign in the ethics of social concern.

THE HARSH REALITY OF PERSISTENT RACISM

On October 22, 1991, the Associated Press ran a story documenting the fact that African Americans and Hispanics were more likely to be rejected for home loans than whites or Asian-Americans, no matter what their income. Because lenders are now required by a provision of the 1989 savings-and-loan bailout law to make reports available to the public, this is the first time such data have been disclosed. The statistics are dramatic. Rejection rates for conventional home mortgage applications were 33.9 percent and 21.4 percent for African Americans and Hispanics, respectively, and 14.4 percent and 12.9 percent for whites and Asian Americans, respectively.[2]

A year later the *Columbus Dispatch* ran a follow-up story targeting the evidence in central Ohio. The results show that in that region African American loan applicants are rejected more than twice as often as white applicants. The denial rate for the former group is 25.3 percent versus 11.9 percent for the latter group.[3]

I suspect that a fair number of people who lived through the remarkable events of the civil rights movement during the 1950s and 1960s and who have seen the opening of new opportunities for ethnic and racial minorities find it difficult to believe that racism remains a major problem in our day. Yet stories like these force us to pause and reconsider—that is, those of us in the white majority need to reconsider, as those belonging to minority groups have not had many illusions about the extent of our progress in race relations. Even though statistics are sometimes deceptive and not always transparent, the dramatic contrasts recorded in the comparative loan denial rates cannot be explained away.

Furthermore, other indicators shake those who underestimate the virulence of racism in our day. In another 1991 study, "focus groups" of young whites in Raleigh, North Carolina, were probed for their feelings about race relations by a professional polling organization. A variety of surprisingly hostile views were expressed by a significant number in the groups. Respondents felt that blacks had an "attitude," chips on their shoulders, and were themselves prejudiced against whites, preferring racial separatism. African Americans were accused of having no work ethic, not taking advantage of their opportunities for advancement, and having too many children. Blacks are quick to claim racism when they lose an election, even when race was not the real cause, according to these whites. Finally, a recurrent theme among the working-class whites sampled is expressed in this quote: "Whatever prejudice whites feel to blacks is provoked by things that blacks do, and whatever prejudice blacks might feel to whites is provoked by something that happened long ago."[4]

The title of the article in which the results of this study of white attitudes are summarized is itself striking: "Just When You Thought It Was the 20th Century...." Unfortunately, this is the twentieth century, the latter days of the century. More important, perhaps, is that the seeds of continued racism in the twenty-first century are now being sown.

A critical sector for the formation of future generations in our society is, of course, the public schools. In his book *Savage Inequalities,* educator and author Jonathan Kozol has painted a grim portrait of the severe inequalities that are evident when the educational opportunities of poor children are contrasted to those of affluent children. In city after city, from coast to coast, Kozol's notebook of facts, firsthand observations, and personal interviews with the disillusioned children of poverty makes clear that, when it comes to the education of our children, things are often not fair. Racism is not the only factor here; it is blended with classism. But racism fuels the injustices of the system, and the injustices of the system help to perpetuate racism.

> The focus in this book is on the inner-city schools; inevitably, therefore, I am describing classrooms in which almost all the children are black or Latino. But there are also poor and mainly white suburban districts and, of course, some desperately poor and very isolated rural districts.... The most important difference in the urban systems, I believe, is that they are often just adjacent to the nation's richest districts, and the ever-present contrast adds a heightened bitterness to the experience of children. The ugliness of racial segregation adds its special injuries as well. It is this killing combination, I believe, that renders life within these urban schools not merely grim but also desperate and often pathological. The fact of destitution is compounded by the sense of being viewed as, somehow, morally infected. The poorest rural schools I've visited feel, simply, bleak. The segregated urban schools feel more like lazarettos.[5]

There are causes of poverty other than racism, and members of racial and ethnic minority groups do not have a corner on the inequities of the economic and educational systems of our society. However, racism is right there in the middle of these inequalities, both historically and in the present. David H. Swinton, dean of the School of Business at Jackson State University offers some familiar observations which make the point:

Throughout American history the economic status of black, Mexican, Puerto Rican, Native American, and other non-European racial or ethnic groups has been significantly lower than that of white Americans. Their economic disadvantage has been indicated by consistently lower levels of income, wealth, business ownership, occupational status, wage rates, and employment and by higher rates of poverty and unemployment.[6]

Moreover, the historical trend continues into the present: Relative gaps in income and poverty rates between blacks and whites have not changed much since the early 1970s, and blacks still receive less than 60 percent of income received by whites and are still roughly three times as likely to be poor in every part of the country.[7]

It is this historically persistent human propensity for prejudice as expressed in racism—and also as expressed in sexism, ageism, and other forms of negative bias—that has been the target of equal opportunity and affirmative action initiatives.

AFFIRMATIVE ACTION BRIEFLY TOLD

In their widely used business ethics textbook, Frederick D. Sturdivant and Heidi Vernon-Wortzel provide a helpful account of the development of contemporary equal opportunity and affirmative action policies. They date the beginnings in the workplace with President Roosevelt's World War II executive order establishing the first fair employment practices committee (FEPC) and prohibiting racial discrimination in employment by companies with federal contracts. However, the FEPC was disbanded at the end of the war, and the large numbers of blacks and women who were hired at the factories while the war was on were then fired to make room for returning white servicemen.[8]

During the 1940s and 1950s, some companies tried to end discrimination in hiring. However, by the early 1960s it was apparent that such voluntary efforts had done little to mitigate the inequities experienced by African Americans and women and by other victims of prejudice as well. Affirmative action was needed. Consequently, Pres. John F. Kennedy issued an executive order in 1961 establishing the President's Commission on Equal Employment Opportunity. The commission was to enforce the basic provision of the executive order to "take affirmative action to ensure that applicants are employed and that employees are treated during employment, without regard to their race, creed, color, or national origin."[9]

The provisions of President Kennedy's executive order were then extended by Title VII of the Civil Rights Act of 1964. In its subsequent amendments in 1972 and 1979, Title VII was extended to cover all employers with fifteen or more employees, with the exception of religious organizations, private clubs, and Native American reservations. While the act prohibited discrimination in hiring, firing, compensation, benefits, and other matters on the basis of race, color, creed, sex, or national origin, it did not require employers to hire or grant preferential treatment on that basis. Actual affirmative action—the phrase coined in President Kennedy's executive order—with the demand for tangible results did not emerge until the 1970 Department of Labor guidelines demanded that federal contractors make good faith efforts to correct deficiencies in the use of minorities and women in their workforces.[10]

In the wake of the Department of Labor guidelines, the Equal Employment Opportunity Commission and the courts both interpreted the Civil Rights Act as having similar provisions and, therefore, extended the affirmative action guidelines to most large employers. Now it was no longer simply a matter of discriminating against a given individual; it was a matter of discriminating against a whole class of people. If women or persons of color or other minority groups were conspicuously absent or relegated to lower-level jobs in the workforce, an employer might be vulnerable to charges of discrimination.[11]

> The law does not require companies to hire unqualified workers. It does require them to go beyond the Civil Rights Act of 1964 and to undertake an active search for qualified minorities, women, and handicapped people to fill positions. Employers are also expected to upgrade the skills and the utilization of these same groups. Affirmative action requires the employer to make as wide a search as possible for qualified applicants and to upgrade present target-group employees.[12]

AFFIRMATIVE ACTION: CONTRIBUTION AND LIMITATION

The reaction to affirmative action has been mixed, even among those whom it is designed to benefit. To continue with the paradigm of the African American situation, we see among African American leaders some decided contrasts in their assessment of the benefits of affirmative action.

Benjamin Hooks, former director of the National Association for the Advancement of Colored People (NAACP), has lashed out against critics of affirmative action, particularly those within the African American community who have been raising the banner of self-help as the antidote to what they fear will be a loss of initiative under the preferential provisions of affirmative action. Although Hooks would hardly argue with the doctrine of hard work and self-improvement, his point is simply that many of the critics would not be in a position to publish their thoughts or have a hearing if affirmative action had not opened up for them positions on university faculties and entrée to respected journals. Affirmative action was needed to help redress the injustices of hundreds of years of oppression and is still needed as long as unfair discrimination lingers.[13] Moreover, there is significant evidence to suggest not only that discrimination lingers but also that affirmative action has had a positive impact on equal employment opportunity.[14]

Typical of the kind of critics Hooks had in his sights is the controversial African American author Shelby Steele, a university English professor who has argued that affirmative action has done more harm than good for African Americans. Among other things, Steele believes that preferential treatment under affirmative action implies inferiority and thereby reinforces historic stereotypes of the innate inferiority of persons of color. This often breeds suspicion among white employers and supervisors that blacks are there because of preferential treatment, not competence. As a consequence, blacks are often prevented from promotion to higher positions. Ironically, the affirmative action policy designed to help them has planted the seeds of a renewed prejudice.[15] I think Steele is simply making the point that government programs to promote or require equality frequently backfire because they do not change the prejudicial hearts of people.

It seems to me that Christians looking at this situation can support Hooks's advocacy of affirmative action policies while yet appreciating the truth of Steele's insights. Reinhold Niebuhr, a giant in Christian ethics in the twentieth century, observed the tendency of groups to put their own self-interest above the needs and even the rights of others. Coercive structures of justice are therefore needed to ensure that a basic level of fairness is promoted—structures, we would add, like the Civil Rights Act and affirmative action rulings. Christian love affirms and supports such justice initiatives, however imperfect and incomplete their achievements, because love seeks the values for the neighbor that justice protects and fosters. At the same time, Christian insight recognizes the persistence of prejudice and racism as expressions of sinful forms of self-interest and, therefore, is realistic about the limits of justice in changing the hearts of people. Consequently, although Christian love finds expression through justice and justice needs the spirit of love, the ideal of love is not fully realized in justice.[16]

However, beyond the lingering tendency toward prejudice and discrimination that always threatens to undermine the structures of justice, affirmative action in practice is bedeviled by an inherent problematic that makes it even more vulnerable to prejudicial impulses. Affirmative action has been designed to correct historic inequities suffered by specific groups of people. In business this means proactive efforts to hire underrepresented groups. It also means ensuring a level playing field in matters of salary and advancement by making those decisions purely on the basis of merit. However, redressing injustice by creating a balanced representation of the diversity of our society at all levels in the workforce and establishing a system of reward based on merit are not always compatible. Some persons may be hired or promoted because they are African American or female *and* qualified, but they may not be the *best* qualified or most meritorious in terms of performance criteria and qualifications. What do you do in the case of a tie? Such circumstances are frequent and inevitable. Backlash is also frequent and inevitable.

Some of this backlash was very evident in the Reagan administration's reversal of equal-employment opportunity and affirmative action enforcement. Administration leaders in the U.S. Department of Justice argued that individuals were unfairly disadvantaged by the preference given to members of groups. The implication is that individual merit has become the victim of quotas, goals, and set-asides.[17]

Is there an ideal that can help us go beyond the limits of affirmative action while preserving its needed benefits? Can we reconsider or reinterpret or supplement the idea of meritorious justice as the equivalent of equalitarian justice in matters of employment, salary, and promotion? Is there a new vision that can breathe the spirit of love into the structures of justice?

BEYOND AFFIRMATIVE ACTION: INDUSTRY AND DIVERSITY

Clearly, guarantees of equal opportunity and affirmative action initiatives will continue to be needed as long as discriminatory practices persist. No one who is concerned for those who suffer the ill effects of prejudice and bias would suggest that these laws have outlived their usefulness. However, those attuned to the demographic changes coming at us recognize that we must move beyond affirmative action and its efforts to help disenfranchised minorities to begin building new communities out of the diversity that will soon characterize the majority.

Almost everyone in business is aware that more than half the present workforce consists of minority-group members, immigrants, and women; native-born white males are a statistical minority, even though they still dominate in terms of power. We are also aware that by the year 2000 white men will account for only 15 percent of the increase in the U.S. workforce. Nonwhite ethnic groups will make up 29 percent of the additions, and as much as 65 percent of women older than 16 will have jobs and constitute nearly 47 percent of the total labor force. Estimates are that the white population will increase little more than 2 percent by century's end, while the Hispanic population is projected to grow by 21 percent, the Asian population by 22 percent, and African Americans by 12 percent. According to an article in *Time* magazine on the occasion of the 1990 census, "By 2056, when someone born today will be 66 years old, the 'average' U.S. resident, as defined by Census statistics, will trace his or her descent to Africa, Asia, the Hispanic world, the Pacific Islands, Arabia—almost anywhere but white Europe."[18] In his *Harvard Business Review* article "From Affirmative Action to Affirming Diversity," R. Roosevelt Thomas Jr. lays out a plan for businesses to maximize the values of the growing diversity in our society and workforce. Thomas is the executive director of the American Institute for Managing Diversity at Morehouse College in Atlanta. The institute's program is an outstanding example of many such programs relating to businesses and other organizations or conducted within corporations themselves. In the face of the developing demographic patterns, Thomas simply points out that having diversity is no longer a choice and affirming it is both just and realistic.[19]

A friend of mine who is a vice-president of human resources commented to me recently that affirmative action did not work because diversity was not valued for its own sake. Instead, businesses got into "the numbers game" and worried about meeting their quotas. This approach bred a certain resentment toward people brought into the company under affirmative action. It is a resentment that is still alive, and he believes it gets in the way of his present training efforts in the area of valuing diversity.

Thomas makes much the same point when he says that we must not repudiate the accomplishments of affirmative action but move beyond it to create an atmosphere in which everyone is valued for what he or she is and brings to the job and in which the diversity of the whole is equally valued. In such an atmosphere all workers would be enabled to do their best with what they bring so that it would be clear that they make a contribution to company success and do not simply represent a concession to some minority. So, Thomas says:

> When we ask how we're doing on race relations, we inadvertently put our finger on what's wrong with the question and with the attitude that underlies affirmative action. So long as racial and gender equality is something we grant to minorities and women, there will be no racial and gender equality. What we must do is create an environment where no one is advantaged or disadvantaged, an environment where "we" is everyone.[20]

A critical step toward building an effective community of diversity that, in business terms, is productive and competitive is to recognize that the old melting-pot notion is no longer viable, if it ever was. The idea that people of many ethnic backgrounds and cultural traditions could be blended together in one prevailing American culture was probably always a popular fiction in our society. In business it was taken much more seriously, however. Corporate success was believed to require a high degree of conformity in which people voluntarily gave up the marks of their particularity. That kind of thinking is no longer possible. Management today and in the future needs to accomplish the same goals of productivity through cultivating diversity that it used to accomplish through enforcing conformity.[21] "The objective is not to assimilate minorities and women into a dominant white male culture but to create a dominant heterogeneous culture."[22]

Certainly, biblical faith provides solid foundations for valuing the dignity and equal worth of each individual. All, we are told, are created in the image of God (Gen. 1:26-27), possessing value that is essentially the gift of creation. Dignity and worth are not the product of our achievements or the accident of our birth; they are innate, inviolable qualities that are bestowed by God. Moreover, our fulfillment in the image of God and the final triumph over the sinful impulses that run counter to its nature are a promise of Christ's victory and a hope of God's final reign (Rom. 8:28-30; 1 Cor. 15:44-49; 2 Cor. 3:18).[23]

In commanding his disciples to love their enemies (Matt. 5:44), Jesus made it clear that there are no qualities that exclude a person from our care and concern, not even malevolence toward us, let alone race, gender, class, or any other accident of birth or life. God, in sending the Christ, John tells us in those familiar words, "loved the world" (John 3:16), the *entire* world, not just one part of it or one group within it. Indeed, Paul tells us that in Christ and in the ultimate dominion of God, "There is no longer Jew or Greek, there is no longer slave or free, there is no longer male and female; for all of you are one in Christ Jesus" (Gal. 3:28). The promise of the gospel is universal in scope and cuts across ethnicity, class, and gender.

Having strong convictions about the equal worth of all persons is one thing, living with the consequences in the practical arrangements of life is, of course, another. In educating for diversity, R. Roosevelt Thomas Jr. says that companies need to clarify their vision of diversity and equal opportunity and work toward a vision that focuses on tapping the full potential of each member of the workforce in an environment where all can do their best because it is not plagued with tensions over issues of equality and the realities of difference. However, he says, "white males, consciously or unconsciously, are likely to cling to a vision that leaves them in the driver's seat."[24]

Change that involves a reordering of power and admits new and different outlooks and styles into full partnership is very threatening. The church is no stranger to this phenomenon. It has often been guilty of prejudicial resistance to change: It has been reluctant to allow a variety of cultural influences to affect theology and practice, it has been slow to allow women their full rights and still has not in some communions, and it has tended to find it more comfortable to cluster and divide according to cultural traditions and class lines than to be fully inclusive. Yet the church has, within its own theology, resources to correct its own failures of vision and something to contribute to the dialogue with those in business who are seeking a new vision in diversity.

Ironically, although the church has often been ambivalent about accepting a diversity of cultural influences in its theology and practice, its own beginning at Pentecost was a powerful demonstration that the gospel of Jesus Christ comes to all people in the language of their own culture. People from every nation under heaven, we are told, were gathered in Jerusalem. The apostles were endowed by the Spirit with the power to speak the gospel message in the native languages of all who were gathered, to the amazement of all who were gathered (Acts 2). The basic intent of the author is doubtless to signal the inauguration of the universal mission of the gospel to all people. It would therefore be hazardous to read into the Pentecost story an argument for contemporary efforts at valuing diversity. Nonetheless, it is significant that the cultural diversity of that era was tacitly affirmed in the use of languages from all known cultures and in the inclusion of those cultures in the one new community of the church.

The fact is that, even in matters of theology and church life, we are all limited by the historical and cultural circumstances that shaped our lives; we receive and express the one universal gospel in and through the manifold experiences of a diverse world. Various insights on the meaning of the one gospel are refracted in the different experiential lenses through which all of us around the world look at it. To see the whole mosaic of divine love for humankind, we need the pieces of many different colors and shapes that we all provide.

However, being open to partnership with and sharing power with those who are different in some significant way are still threatening. Will we lose control? Will our own cherished patterns and traditions be compromised and even lost? These are deeply personal issues of security. Will diversity and pluralism in an organization lead to chaos in both thought and action? Will the tensions caused by differences tear us apart? These are issues of institutional anxiety.

When white men in the business world, who have enjoyed doing things their way for as long as anyone can remember, feel threatened by the influences of ethnic and gender diversity at work, they resemble their counterparts in the pew who fear that they will lose their most beloved hymns to African American spirituals or rock music versions of the liturgy that they can neither sing nor understand. However, the same Spirit of Pentecost, who affirmed and used human cultural diversity, provides through the gospel the wherewithal to live with it.

To begin with, the message of the gospel the Spirit mediates is one of freedom. The word that in Christ God accepts us as we are through no merit or accomplishment of our own frees us from fear for our own security. When our hope is in the promise of God's unconditional grace, we can be open to genuine community with those who are different and whose presence means change.

Knowing that our only hope is in the grace of God and not in anything we have done clues us in to the fact that no particular institutions, traditions, customs, practices, or "ways of doing things" are sacred; only God's promise is sacred. Therefore, we are free to be critical of existing institutions and practices and to experiment with change. To make absolute one way of doing things or one way of thinking is idolatrous. Only God's promise in Christ is absolute.

In the Bible, a sure sign of the coming God's final reign is the outpouring of the Spirit. The manifestation of the Spirit at Pentecost is further confirmation of the message of Christ's Easter victory that, in him, the promise of God's dominion of life, love, and harmony is both revealed and assured. Until that dominion is present in its fullness, we will struggle with division and differences, and we will often fail. But to struggle to forge a community of diversity in which all are valued as they are and for what they are is to anticipate the promise of God's reign.

To the extent that we begin to see both intrinsic and practical values in building an organizational team that reflects the diversity of the larger culture and the emerging international business culture, we can shed new light on the inherent problematic of affirmative action that I mentioned before: Assuring diversity at all levels of the workforce and rewarding people on the basis of merit alone—two goals of affirmative action—are not always compatible. The problem is merit. Criteria of merit tend to be quantitative and oriented toward the bottom line and performance: volume of sales, billable hours, numbers of publications, successful grant applications, cost reduction, and efficiency standards. There is no question that such measures are important to any competitive organization. However, if we have a vision of the inherent value of diversity in a world of diversity, we can add to these rather "objective" meritorious considerations those of a person's "contribution" to the values of diversity.

In the standard accounts of distributive justice, contribution stands alongside merit as a basis for justly distributing the good. To hire or reward persons not only because they are capable in terms of merit but also because they contribute to diversity in an organization makes ethical sense. As it happens, it also make business sense: The company that reflects the composition of the society at all its levels is likely to be the company best attuned to that society, its needs, and its desires. As my friend in human resources put it, when you talk about the "best" person for a job, you have to look at the whole person and the whole person in the context of society, not just certain achievements.

Cornel West, one of the leading African American thinkers of our time, has a noteworthy chapter in *Race Matters*, "Beyond Affirmative Action: Equality and Identity." West observes—basically as we have—that affirmative action is a necessary but limited project. Its impact is primarily a negative one: to prevent the rampant discrimination that would likely occur in its absence. Affirmative action does relatively little to ameliorate central problems of black poverty and identity or self-worth.[25]

However, as West makes clear elsewhere in the book, if we look at this as the problem of African Americans, we are doomed to perpetuate the racism that so deeply infects all our institutions. The problem is *our* problem as a flawed American society and culture. We are all in it together. Therefore, West maintains, we need leaders, black and white, who can focus on the common good and the achievement of a truly democratic, multiracial society.[26] I would hope that the valuing and cultivation of diversity we have been discussing are steps in that direction.

It is time to glimpse some of the "contributions" that come from cultivating diversity, in this case gender diversity.

BEYOND AFFIRMATIVE ACTION: THE QUEST FOR A WORKABLE ANDROGYNY

At the end of 1992, the *Washington Post National Weekly Edition* reported that well-educated women have made great strides in professional and executive occupations.[27] The statistics are impressive, suggesting that at least in this area of the workforce women are moving rapidly toward equality.

However, some studies still indicate that women earn less than men for comparable work, on the average, for all occupations, and the same *Post* story also tells us that less-educated women remain stuck in low-paying jobs in child care and office work because they are unable to break into the male-dominated blue-collar jobs that pay well.[28] Clearly, there is affirmative action work that needs to be done on this front for women.

Nonetheless, for the present, I want to look at that arena in which

things are going decidedly better for women, the more lucrative professional and executive ranks. Moving beyond affirmative action in the
sense of equal opportunity and greater parity in the numbers, I want to
ask whether the increased numbers and success of women in business
and professional life have brought about increased openness to the gifts
and traits of character that women bring with them from their particular
histories. Have women merely been increasingly *included,* or has the
workplace become a more *inclusive* place where the special contributions
of women are valued for their enrichment of a diverse working team?

Recent studies have confirmed what many have known from experience, that organizations that have been established, managed, and dominated by men have been characterized by decision-making processes,
communication patterns, and norms of interaction that are based on
what is normative for the male experience and outlook. Specifically,
men place a strong emphasis on work and achievement and little emphasis on emotional involvement with others. Consequently, relationships at
work are often seen as bridges to personal success, which should be
attained as early in the career as possible. Because work and achievement
define male identity, traits like competitiveness, aggressiveness, task orientation, and emotional control are important to cultivate.[29] Not surprisingly, the features of this male portrait bear a striking resemblance to
the features of corporate culture portrayed by Robert Jackall, whose
work was discussed in the early chapters.

By contrast, studies of women show that women give priority to relationships. Consequently, women have a tendency to assist others in
reaching their goals and to emphasize the importance of intimate relationships over personal achievement. Both of these traits are consistent
with women's tendencies to define themselves in relation to others and
to be more comfortable with self-disclosure and the development of
close personal relationships.[30]

To the extent that these differences have been recognized, they have
often been used against women as they entered into competition for
leadership positions in business. Wittingly or unwittingly, both men and
women in business have tended to develop the stereotype of the ideal
manager in terms of traits more common to men. The contrasting or
complementary traits of women have then been used to stereotype them
as lacking the task-oriented skills necessary for leadership and, in general, as not having the right combination of qualities to assume leadership
positions. These stereotypical perceptions have prevailed, even though
performance records do not show them to be valid. Indeed, some
women leaders have actually been closer to the stereotype of the ideal
leader than many of their male counterparts![31]

In a sense, the fact that many women in leadership positions do, in fact, approximate the male-informed stereotype of the ideal leader is *the* problem for some, including Suzanne Gordon, who points out that, initially, feminists entering the business world did so with the conviction that compassion and competition were not incompatible. They hoped to bring *caring* into the workplace as a corrective to the highly individualistic, independent ethos of competitiveness that had characterized the male-dominated business culture. However, that agenda has almost disappeared: "Today many women—particularly younger ones—do not even remember this powerful feminist vision of social transformation. That's because the feminism that dominates the news and public debates is a brand of feminism that teaches us to adopt and adapt to male marketplace values, activities, and beliefs. That's what equal opportunity feminism is all about."[32]

This adaptive feminism, so congenial to mainstream society, Gordon calls "equal opportunity feminism" and credits it with reshaping feminism and women in masculine contours. A new breed of woman—economic or acquisitive woman—has emerged with the traits of detachment, aggressive competitiveness, and lust for success that have characterized the male-dominated culture of work. In Gordon's mind "equal opportunity" is a notion that connotes the kind of personal, upward mobility dream that leads people to the sort of dispassionate disconnectedness required for success in a competitive world. "Equality," she believes, is a contrasting notion that suggests community.[33]

There is, I think, a correlation here with our previous discussion of diversity. There we observed that building community in diversity is a sign of equality in a pluralistic world. However, the way we have dealt with affirmative action by stressing the overriding importance of *individual* merit or performance success as the key to equal opportunity and equal rewards distracts our attention from the communitarian values that are also at stake in affirmative action. The message seems clear. To the extent that we stress personal gain over inclusive community, our efforts at an equalitarian workplace or society will always be bedeviled by the kind of competition that continually creates haves and have-nots and, sometimes, exacerbates racism and sexism.

In any case, a society dominated by ambition for personal success and material gain makes workaholics of increasing numbers of people and drastically reduces our ability and opportunities to care. For women in business and in other arenas of life, it is essential, Gordon maintains, to reclaim the earlier feminist agenda to create a caring culture. It is a matter of restructuring lives and priorities so that career and caring can coexist. Caring for aged parents, being involved in the lives and activities of children, and contributing to a society that can sustain all its members should again be integral parts of life, along with career goals and material ambitions.[34]

A bit of flexibility and creativity on the part of companies can help create space for caring. However, Gordon insists, to change the corporate culture requires that women stand up for their caring commitments and challenge policies that make excessive demands on employees' time or refuse to make accommodation to their legitimate needs. Taking this stance means reclaiming the contribution that women can make out of their caregiving experience. They need to liberate themselves from the need to accommodate. But, in the final analysis, it is not women's liberation we are talking about; it is human liberation.[35]

Perhaps there is hope for Gordon's vision yet. I had a marvelous talk with an African American woman who is a bank branch manager in a large Midwestern city. One of her more memorable comments seems to fit here. She said that she believed that women in business were helping to humanize the workplace, "especially since they're now starting to behave like women!" And, of course, as Gordon herself recognizes, there are plenty of men ready to join the ranks of women in promoting an ethos of care, just as there have been plenty of women ready to join the ranks of men in an ethos of competition.

Compassion and competition are neither mutually exclusive nor necessarily peculiar to one gender, even though they may predominate culturally in one gender or the other. Openness to the contribution of each gender in a working community in which diversity is valued, as we earlier described it, can help all concerned discover new resources and possibilities for their personal development and for the corporate performance as well.

Returning for a moment to our earlier theme of diversity in community, we find, in the matter of gender diversity as well, that valuing diversity not only affirms all individuals in their own particularity but also places everyone in a situation where they can learn to rise above their own limits and learn new possibilities from others. Thus, gender diversity helps to promote *androgyny,* the ability of members of each gender to blend traits characteristically associated with both genders. Indeed, studies show that androgynous leaders in business tend to be the most effective managers, whether male or female. Theologian James Nelson has some comments on the idea of androgyny that help bring us to a close:

> The concept of androgyny has been commonplace for some years. Most simply put, it denotes the integration within a single person of traits traditionally identified by gender stereotypes as masculine and as feminine. Thus, androgynous people characterize themselves both as strongly self-reliant, assertive and independent, and as strongly understanding, affectionate and compassionate. Androgyny is an appealing alternative to the

oppressiveness of gender role stereotypes. It goes beyond the false dualism of the belief that there are certain inherent personality traits of male and of female. It moves us beyond oppressive gender expectations into the possibility of a more genuinely human liberation for each and for all.[36]

Whether it is the battle against racism and for the values of a more diverse business community or the battle against sexism and the restoration of a caring community through fostering a healthy androgyny, Christians can easily recognize the need for agape to influence the culture of caring and for that same love to seek the equality of each person in community as a witness to the ultimate community of love in God's promised reign.

Christians also should recognize that equal opportunity and affirmative action benefit only those who are able and have the economic and educational advantages to prepare themselves for a career in business. To move beyond affirmative action to caring and community in business means moving toward caring and community in society at large. It means raising questions of the role of business in this social transformation, questions of corporate responsibility for public education and economic justice. These are questions we will address to some degree in the final two chapters.

8

BEYOND MERE SURVIVAL

Calling for global responsibility is first and foremost the opposite of calling for what is a mere ethic of success: It is the opposite of an action for which the end sanctifies the means and for which whatever functions, brings profit, power or enjoyment, is good.... So in concrete terms, the slogan for the Third Millennium should run: World society is responsible for its own future! This is responsibility for our society and environment and also for the world after us.[1]

So stated noted theologian Hans Küng. In Küng's views the world will have a future only if we develop a universal ethic of responsibility for the world and for each other, responsibility that includes care for the environment, an outlook on nature that is more than simplistically utilitarian.

It is hard to imagine an arena of ethical concern more suited to the sort of dialogue we have been trumpeting than the environment. By its very nature, the present crisis of the environment is on everyone's agenda. Therefore, it should not be surprising to see it as a central issue of Küng's concern for the responsible global society of the future. However, everyone's agenda does not necessarily classify environmental issues as ethical. Everyone has heard the alarm that, if we do not change our ways, the effects of pollution, global warming, depletion of the ozone layer, and overpopulation will threaten our survival as a race and the viability of the biosphere itself. In response to this threat, we have promoted legislation, technology, research, and new ways of thinking about how industry can expand in environmentally responsible ways. These initiatives are essential components for an effective environmentalism, but they do not, by themselves, constitute an ethic for the environment. Rather, government regulation, scientific and technological projects, and plans for responsible industrial expansion are parts of a strategy for survival.

It is the contention of this chapter that a strategy for survival is necessary but not sufficient. We need to move beyond the necessities for survival to an ethic that values and cares for the whole of nature, even as we value and care for the well-being of humankind, an ethic in which nature has intrinsic as well as instrumental value. Practically speaking, if nature has only instrumental value (useful material for some human purpose), a commitment to care for it is always susceptible to change as shifts occur in our sense of the urgency of environmental problems. Our perspectives and our actions can easily change under the sway of new scientific studies or complex economic and political pressure, if our concern for nature is not anchored in some sense of its intrinsic value. Establishing the intrinsic value of nature is not an easy task, however; it involves a major paradigm shift for most people, even those who love nature and value its beauty and preservation.

There is evidence that at least some leaders in industry have begun to appreciate the need for this change in paradigms. E. S. Woolard, CEO of DuPont, in a speech on corporate environmentalism, pointed out that industry has, through research and production, a special capacity and responsibility to make a more significant contribution to an environmentally sound future than any other sector of society. "However," said Woolard, "industry will only fulfill that role if it adopts certain ethical principles now and continues to abide by them in the years ahead. The critical step is for industry to value the natural world as more than a source of raw material and a receptacle for waste."[2] These words are an encouraging sign of a growing environmental wisdom among leaders in business. Despite the kind of ethical insight expressed by Woolard and, as we shall see, an explosion of environmental consciousness in business, however, there is still a long way to go in developing an ethic for environmentalism.

It is the further contention of this chapter that moving beyond immediate pressures of survival to a more foundational environmental ethic is one of the areas of ethics in business where the church and church people in business can make a strong contribution.

In what follows we will have a kind of dialogue between the insights of Christian faith and ethics and the strategies of business with respect to the environment. It is yet another instance illustrative of the dialogue that I have been advocating.

AN UNHOLY ALLIANCE?

For many, the prospect of church and industry in dialogue for a stronger environmentalism is strange indeed. After all, there is considerable historical evidence to link the teaching of the church and the growth of industry with the development of the very attitudes and practices that have gotten us into our environmental problems.

In his book *The Travail of Nature,* H. Paul Santmire characterizes what he calls "the ecological critique of Christianity" by sampling a number of influential voices from inside and outside theology. The complaint of these various critics is fairly constant: Christian faith and vision have been overwhelmingly preoccupied with concern for the salvation of humankind. In this anthropocentric view of things, nature is merely a part of the scenery for the human drama. As a consequence, there has been little in the way of resources for a strong environmental ethic. On the contrary, some would claim that the roots of our irresponsible behavior toward the environment are to be found in the neglect, if not the disdain, of the Christian tradition for the natural order. Indeed, Santmire concedes that even those contemporary theologians and ethicists who advocate environmental responsibility do so from an anthropocentric perspective. Typically, they stress "responsible stewardship" of the environment, which, notwithstanding its respect for all of nature, is nonetheless a model that places humanity in a paternalistic position over against nature.[3]

Although Santmire admits that the critics have a point, the burden of his historical study is to demonstrate that the orientation of Christian tradition toward nature is ambiguous rather than uniform. There are certainly influential theologies in which nature is but a footnote, but there are other examples, equally influential, in which all of nature is included in a vision of cosmic salvation. Origen and Aquinas illustrate the former; Augustine and Francis of Assisi illustrate the latter. Origen's deep suspicion and disdain for nature stand in stark contrast to Francis's deep sense of communion with nature; Augustine's vision of creation as expressive of the overflowing goodness of God finds its counterpoint in Aquinas's subordination of the natural and historical and elevation of the spiritual and the eternal. These examples are matched by numerous other examples of the tradition, which, in their contrasting motifs regarding the natural world, express the ambiguity of the tradition that Santmire has discovered.[4]

For Santmire, the ambiguity of the tradition suggests that there *are* positive models on which to build an environmental ethic. Moreover, contemporary biblical studies have also been opening up new avenues for recasting the Christian contribution to an ethic for the environment. Although Christians should take their critics seriously and strive to do better, there is no reason to consider Christian theology environmentally bankrupt, and the distortions of the tradition should not deflect us from the enormous resources our faith provides.

Christian ethicist James A. Nash has listened to the same critical voices as has Paul Santmire and basically agrees with his analysis of the Christian tradition. In fact, Nash is able to find some additional examples of figures in the Christian tradition whose piety, spirituality, and doctrine included a deep respect for the whole creation. Like Santmire, he acknowledges a certain validity to many of the criticisms directed against the environmental sensibilities of the Christian tradition. However, he also sees the tradition as ambiguous rather than consistent and argues forcefully that other religious traditions have a similar record; there is no need to demonize Christianity as the historical archenemy of environmentalism. With Santmire, Nash sees the possibilities in the resources of Christian teaching and tradition for reformation and strong contribution to environmental ethics.[5] We shall spend most of this chapter dwelling on the sorts of positive possibilities Nash and Santmire see for the Christian witness in environmental ethics. However, before moving further in that direction, we need to look at the linkage between Christian thought and industrial development that was mentioned earlier.

As is well known, the emphasis of the great reformers Martin Luther and John Calvin was on human salvation, God's gracious condescension to a sinful humanity. This emphasis, as much as any other in the history of Christian thought, placed the cause of nature in the background and hid the ecological treasures of theology behind a veil of heightened anthropocentrism. Moreover, when Calvin blended this anthropocentric focus with his peculiar stress on the sovereignty of God, he produced a theology of vocation in which God's elect reflect divine sovereignty in their dominion over nature, reshaping the world to the glory of God. This, says Santmire, "helps set the stage, among many other factors, for later—secularized—developments in Western mercantile and industrial society and its ethic of domination over the earth."[6]

Despite these powerful trends in Reformation thought, there still were some value and hope for the whole of creation being expressed theologically, at least on the periphery of the reformers' thought. Luther, in particular, had a keen sense of the wonders of God's creative activity in nature. He maintained that the redeemed begin to see nature anew, and their experience of God's grace opens up the beauty of the whole world to them. In fact, Luther looks forward to the divine consummation of creation at the very end of time, when there will be a transformation of all things and we—we and the whole creation—will be more beautiful than ever before. To be sure, these thoughts are a minor chord in Luther's work, but they are there nonetheless.[7]

However, even this Reformation glance in the direction of nature was averted in the modern era by the combined secular influences of the natural sciences, philosophy, and modern industrialism. The mechanical view of the universe promoted by the science and philosophy of the time combined with the rise of industrialism to create a view of nature as a mere world of objects to be used and manipulated and exploited for human interests, a world that human beings transcended and dominated. Protestant thought increasingly isolated humanity from nature in its thinking and thought it appropriate to humanity's special relationship with God that people endeavor to transcend nature and control it. The weak link between concern for humanity and concern for nature in Reformation theology was thereby snapped.[8]

It is difficult to analyze with certainty just how trends in a given time interact to produce certain results. It is probably most accurate to say that theology basically stood aside and allowed science, philosophy, and industry to promote a secularized version of a mechanical view of nature. Through its anthropocentricity and its neglect of a theology of nature, Christian tradition doubtlessly influenced or paved the way for a secular view of human domination and control over nature. However, as the secular, mechanical view of the natural world developed, theology simply abdicated responsibility for nature and history and made the relationship of God and humanity the sole focus of its interest.[9]

Although confession is good for the soul, and both church and industry have many environmental sins to confess, what is of greater interest to us are the way in which both are now moving toward a more responsible environmental ethic and the way in which the dialogue between the perspectives of Christianity and industry can be a helpful contribution to the emerging new environmentalism. Christianity and industry are looking for and discovering resources in their respective traditions that can help to develop a stronger culture of responsibility for the environment.

BEYOND DEVELOPMENT
TO SUSTAINABLE DEVELOPMENT

During the first two weeks of June 1992, the second Earth Summit, officially known as the United Nations Conference on Environment and Development (UNCED), was convened in Rio de Janeiro. A global forum was also convened by nongovernmental organizations (NGOs) at the same time and place. These two events, attended by delegates from 178 countries and by 188 heads of state and government, drew some 35,000 attendees, of whom nearly 9,000 were reporters from all branches of the media. By consensus, the delegates at UNCED accepted the Rio Declaration on Environment and Development, which set forth policy principles governing the rights, responsibilities, and relationships of nations in promoting sustainable development through a new global partnership.

Through this massive global event the notion of sustainable development has been imprinted on the environmental consciousness of the world. There are a number of definitions of sustainable development and considerable disagreement over what policies and practices actually represent sustainable development. However, the gist of it is that the necessary growth and development of the world's economy must be governed by a commitment to sustainability, the policy and practice of preserving the earth's resources for future generations and future development. The concept of sustainability directs our concern toward safeguarding the self-renewing capacity of natural systems and toward reducing our reliance on nonrenewable resources. The idea of development, of course, comprehends the need for economically developed nations to continue developing wealth and economic opportunity and for economically underdeveloped nations to grow toward greater and greater parity. The principle or concept of sustainable development, then, combines the two needs into a single vision projecting the necessity and hope that the natural order and the socioeconomic order can thrive together.

The idea of sustainable development, of course, was not born at Rio in June 1992. The problem of environmental degradation on the part of the industrialized world has long been discussed in connection with the plight of the Third World, both in terms of the global economic injustice involved and in terms of the environmental cost of redressing that injustice through greater economic development in the poorer countries. However, what is perhaps a genuinely recent development is the proactive stance of international business in embracing the concept of sustainable development as a guide to corporate environmental responsibility.

In the Summer 1992 issue of *Conservation Exchange,* the National Wildlife Federation's publication for corporate leaders, the lead article detailed how sustainable development has begun to influence the way multinational corporations approach doing business in developing countries. This contributes a virtual paradigm shift among international business leaders, who now see the connection between their business agenda and responsible participation in vital global issues such as the environment. The article goes on to illustrate the point by describing how an impressive number of business organizations, involving corporations from North America, Europe, and Asia, have organized to address issues of sustainable development in global business.[10]

As might be expected, the National Wildlife Federation itself has become deeply involved in the issue of sustainable development. The January 1992 conference held by the National Wildlife Federation Corporate Conservation Council published a report, "Building the Sustainable Corporation." Out of the conference came a number of principles for ensuring sustainable development and building a sustainable enterprise. The report sets forth principles that address steps industry can take in achieving ecological security, resource security, and socioeconomic security, the three basic components of sustainable development.

Ecological security involves measures of protecting, preserving, and restoring nature's ecosystems. This means pollution prevention and control, land use management, reforestation, and reclamation, to name a few obvious examples.

Resource security deals with concern for nonrenewable natural resources. Economizing through miniaturization, insulation, and aerodynamics; conservation through recycling, reconditioning, and mass transit and; finally, substitution of renewable resources for nonrenewable resources are examples of many efforts under way toward resource security.

The third goal, achieving socioeconomic security, brings themes of global, social, and economic justice into the equation. Through techniques such as technology transfer, credit extension, minority employment, and human services such as primary health care, family planning, urban transport, and primary education, business and industry can help to foster a better standard of living and better economic development in the Two-Thirds World.[11] This is but a snapshot of one piece of the report, but it gives us an idea of the kinds of things that are involved on the agenda of sustainable development when corporations start thinking about their role.

Among the most impressive reports published in preparation for the Rio summit was *Changing Course,* written by Stephen Schmidheiny and Lloyd Timberlake for the Business Council for Sustainable Development (BCSD). The council, comprised of leaders of large corporations throughout the world, has lifted up the challenge to business to participate with governments and environmentalists in creating a new and practical vision for sustainable development in the future:

> Sustainable development requires forms of progress that meet the needs of the present without compromising the ability of future generations to meet their own needs. In the late twentieth century, we are failing in the first clause of that definition by not meeting the basic needs of more than one billion people. We have not even begun to come to grips with the second clause: the needs of future generations. Some argue that we have no responsibility for the future, as we cannot know its needs. This is partly true. But it takes no great leap of reason to assume that our offspring will require breathable air, drinkable water, productive soils and oceans, a predictable climate, and abundant plant and animal species on the planet they will share.[12]

The BCSD report goes on to deal with a number of the same dimensions of sustainable development explored in the National Wildlife

Federation report. It also includes some important reflections on how to integrate environmental responsibility with corporate decision making and planning and how the market forces of the free enterprise system can be harnessed for promoting a more responsible environmentalism.

FROM STRATEGY TO ETHICS

Reports like these and others we could name, along with countless books and articles about the environment, provide detailed discussion of elaborate and extensive economic and political strategies, scientific pursuits, and technological developments. They are of enormous practical importance for our ability to deal effectively with the challenge of the environment. However, strategic planning and scientific progress do not constitute an ethical framework. For an environmental strategy to succeed and endure, it must be built upon ethical foundations that are themselves enduring. In the absence of such ethical foundations, business leaders and other leaders will constantly be tempted to ask why it is necessary to expend resources and take risks on behalf of environmental responsibility. And, in the absence of clear ethical commitments, the answer to that question will likely be that it is necessary only when it is required by law or profitable as a response to the latest developments in public opinion.

The question of whether an environmental strategy is firmly rooted in an environmental ethic and whether corporations need such an ethic to ensure their environmental responsibility is not unrelated to a critical question of ethics in business that we have already discussed. I have in mind the now recurrent question of whether the moral responsibility of corporations extends beyond the "moral minimum" with respect to social concerns in general and, now, concerns with the environment in particular.

In a recent issue of *Business Ethics Quarterly,* W. Michael Hoffman, founding director of the Center for Business Ethics at Bentley College, wrote an article on business and environmental ethics in which he challenged the position that companies have no responsibility beyond the moral minimum. Specifically, Hoffman was attacking the view of well-known business ethicist Norman Bowie, who along with others, has maintained that business has no obligation to protect or enhance the environment beyond what is required by law. At the same time, Bowie says, business should not attempt to quash legislation on behalf of the environment through its lobbying efforts.[13]

Bowie's concern in these two points is to avoid two extremes of corporate behavior. The first is the kind of corporate suicide that would occur if a company were to adopt environmental policies so far ahead of the curve as to make it unprofitable and threaten its existence. The other extreme is to be so self-interested as to set corporate profits over against public well-being. To avoid such extremes, one should simply adhere to the moral minimum, which in Bowie's definition is compliance with what is legally required. However, Hoffman contends that the business ethics movement during the past fifteen years has taught us that business has a responsibility "to become a more active partner in dealing with social concerns. Business must creatively find ways to become a part of solutions, rather than being a part of problems. Corporations can and must develop a conscience, as Kenneth Goodpaster and others have argued—and this includes an environmental conscience."[14]

To call for an environmental conscience presumes that conscience is informed by an authentic environmental ethic that embodies genuine commitments to the care of the earth and the common good, however. Therefore, Hoffman questions the kind of rhetoric and thinking that market good ethics as good business and convey the attractive idea that good reports on a corporation's environmental responsibility will translate to good quarterly reports to its stockholders. Hoffman argues, "Is the rationale that good ethics is good business a proper one for business ethics? I think not. One thing that the study of ethics has taught us over the past twenty-five hundred years is that being ethical may on occasion require that we place the interests of others ahead of or at least on a par with our own interests. And this implies that the ethical thing to do, the morally right thing to do may not be in our own self-interest."[15]

Certainly all that we have said about how the Christian ethic of agape goes the extra mile places us squarely in Hoffman's corner on this particular issue. Moreover, in chapter 4, where I attempted to give a theological-ethical account of the place of business in the world, we located business among the "orders of vocation and anticipation." These are the institutions and venues of human activity that God has providentially established for the common good and in which Christians live out their vocation through that ethic of love. From this vantage point, it seems to me that Christians have a genuine stake in advocating a business ethos that goes beyond the moral minimum in matters of urgent social concern.

To be sure, as we have observed before, motivations for this posture within business and industry will be a mixed bag, including some inauthentic reasons such as Hoffman has cited. However, while the recognition of this reality preserves us from naive visions of moral progress, it does not deter us from making a strong Christian witness on behalf of the environment, urging attention to the establishment of ethical foundations for environmental responsibility, and supporting environmentally friendly policies and practices wherever they may emerge for whatever reason.

Once again, as Reinhold Niebuhr has taught us, justice through coercion and balance of power may not be a morally lofty achievement, but it is better than injustice, and Christians should get behind that and push. Similarly, environmental responsibility motivated by the promise of better profits and better public image, not to mention legal sanctions, may not be a lofty moral achievement either, but it is better than unrestrained environmental degradation.

The BCSD report *Changing Course* does not have a listing for ethics in its index, although the implications of the report for environmental ethics are enormous. And, in at least one place, the discussion diverges from a causal analysis of business and economic forces to suggest that our commitments to a better earth are at the bottom of real progress in environmentalism. Schmidheiny points out in this instance that the prevention of pollution is finally a matter of desire, a notion that has more depth of moral significance than commonplace expediency. He quotes Paul R. Wilkinson of DuPont: "Source [pollutants] reduction is more than an economic incentive or a compliance requirement. It is a priority for environmental stewardship against which we must continually measure our performance."[16]

By contrast, the absence of solid ethical foundations for environmental responsibility opens up the temptation to back off from environmental commitments. Not only might the pressures of profitability exert an adverse influence, but changing and uncertain data from scientific studies often provide leverage against needed reforms. Not long ago, at a public forum on environmental ethics, a corporate attorney asked me the pointed question as to why industry should make sacrifices to reduce the sources of global warming when scientific data were ambiguous on the real threat of global warming. It was a rhetorical question. Similarly, an environmental officer of a utilities company with whom I recently worked argued that environmental ethics have been given undue prominence among ethical issues in the public mind, especially when studies such as the one on acid rain in the late 1980s seemed to demonstrate that there is less problem than we thought.

The need for business to find solid ethical foundations on which to build environmental policies and practices reminds one of a familiar parable of Jesus which, in Matthew's Gospel, comes at the end of the Sermon on the Mount:

> "Everyone then who hears these words of mine and acts on them will be like a wise man who built his house on rock. The rain fell, the floods came, and the winds blew and beat on that house, but it did not fall, because it had been founded on rock. And everyone who hears these words of mine and does not act on them will be like a foolish man who built his house on sand. The rain fell, and the floods came, and the winds blew and beat against that house, and it fell—and great was its fall!" (Matt. 7:24-27)[17]

It is tempting to take this parable and mold it and stretch it to fit our present purpose. Such an imaginative interpretation might point out that environmental policies and practices that are not founded on solid ethics will be like the house built on sand. As soon as the gathering clouds of market forces and short-term losses get stirred up by the shifting winds of scientific opinions that appear to diminish the environmental crisis, we can have a storm brewing that will wash away the edifice of environmental responsibility. Policies and practices founded on solid ethics, however, are like the house built on a rock, able to withstand threats and temptations and stay with a course that is best for the earth and for human society alike.

Of course, such an interpretation was hardly in the mind of Jesus or Matthew. Jesus was calling upon those who heard his teaching to recognize that he was the Messiah, the one who was bringing in God's dominion and the fulfillment of all the promises associated with that final reign of God. Jesus is the rock on which to build. Indeed, it is not even the teaching of Jesus that is the solid foundation, but Jesus himself as the bearer of the promise of salvation for the whole world. For Jesus and for us who follow him, ethics are built on hope on God's promise, not on hope in our own efforts.[18]

If this is the real meaning of the parable, then our previous application of it to contemporary issues of the environment is indeed far-fetched. However, when we recognize that environmental ethics and ethics in general arise out of fundamental beliefs about the meaning and hope of life, we can begin to see that for business leaders to develop an adequate environmental ethic to sustain responsible policies and practices, they will need to get in touch with basic convictions about the value of the earth and all that is in it, about its nature and hope for its destiny. While hope in Christ and the earth ethic that follows is profoundly different from other hopes based in human imaginings, the need for hope and the capacity to hope are the common impulse in all. Once that is understood, applying the parable is not so far-fetched after all, and Christians, in talking about the rock on which they build, can make a contribution to that quest.

AN ETHIC OF VALUE:
DISCERNING THE GOOD IN HOPE

In W. Michael Hoffman's argument for an authentic ethic of environmental responsibility for business, the key issue turns out to be whether we regard the nonhuman world as something that has intrinsic value (value in itself). If the natural world, living and nonliving, has only instrumental value (value based on its usefulness to human beings), then there will be no ultimate moral constraint to protect nature from degradation or extinction and no impetus to restore it to wholeness when possible. If nature has only instrumental value and the interest of human beings is the measure of all things, it is hard to see how business can adopt ethics that go beyond the moral minimum and beyond self-interest. Hoffman charges that, just as people are marketing business ethics because it is good for business, they are also marketing environmental ethics as in the human interest. Neither of these approaches represents authentic approaches to ethics.[19]

Eugene C. Hargrove, in his *Foundations of Environmental Ethics,* offers a view similar to Hoffman's. Hargrove contends that unless we have grounds for asserting the intrinsic value of natural objects and species as a protection against their economic exploitation, we cannot have environmental ethics of any sort.[20] Hargrove speaks as a philosopher looking for a basis in the history of Western thought upon which to build environmental ethics in which the natural world is endowed with intrinsic goodness. In his examination of various movements in Western thought, he believes that he has found that basis.[21] The distinguished environmentalist, Holmes Rolston III takes the matter a step further. Rolston believes that he can make a case on naturalistic, rational grounds for the intrinsic value of species and ecosystems. He goes on from there to develop ethics for the environment and for business in relationship to the environment based on this premise.[22]

Efforts such as those of Hargrove and Rolston are important to the overall dialogue because they represent secular arguments with which Christian perspectives can connect in the kind of pluralistic dialogue that has been described throughout this discussion. Just as we saw that beneficence is a notion helpful to communicating some of the meaning that Christians place upon agape, arguments like those of Hargrove and Rolston are complementary to a Christian theology that asserts the intrinsic value of creation as a basis for its environmentalism.

However, although we may be grateful for dialogue partners such as Hargrove and Rolston, as Hargrove himself points out, philosophy has not often been a friend to the environment. Despite his claims to find a basis for environmentalism in the history of Western thought, Hargrove also believes that philosophy has, from the Greeks to the present, been anthropocentric in its orientation. Philosophy has looked upon nature and its value primarily in terms of its usefulness for the human enterprise. In this regard, Hargrove notes that, although religion is often criticized as antienvironmental, philosophy is far more the culprit and has had a far more pervasive influence upon attitudes, at least in Western culture!²³ In any case, making the argument for some sense of the intrinsic value of nature as a cornerstone for an environmental ethic will be no mean feat, given this bias of our Western culture. Indeed, even the most enlightened advocates of environmentalism continue to operate with anthropocentric arguments. The following quotation from the National Wildlife Federation's *Building the Sustainable Corporation* suggests that it is, finally, human well-being that is the motive force for environmental responsibility: "Attaining ecological security for the planet demands that we *protect* certain vital ecosystems by minimizing their degradation; preserve the critical ecosystem-services *that support humankind;* and restore degraded ecosystems to productivity so they may *benefit the earth's economies and expanding population.*"²⁴

Again, Christian realism like that of a Niebuhr would certainly want to assert that anthropocentric environmental ethics that help to preserve the environment are far better than no environmental ethics at all. Furthermore, Christians would be forced to recognize, as environmentalists are as well, that concerns for human need and the needs of nature are continually intermingled, often in conflictual ways, and the claims of both are intrinsically valid. For Christians the challenge is to project environmental ethics that establish the intrinsic value of nature as well as the intrinsic value of the human good and work toward a comprehensive system of justice for people and justice for the environment that can help to inform the vision of sustainable development in the world of business and industry.

In that regard, the first challenge is to establish ethics of value that include the intrinsic value of nature, ethics that reverse the supposed anthropocentricity of the Christian tradition. We do not have the space to be exhaustive in this effort, but we can certainly offer some key themes:

1. In the Bible, the world of nature is of God's making, and it enjoys the unqualified blessing of the Creator: "God saw everything that he had made and, indeed, it was very good" (Gen. 1:31a).

2. Although human beings, created in the image of God, are singled out as preeminent in the creation narrative of Genesis 1, this preeminence is not a license to exploit the earth. Rather, integral to the personhood that is at the core of the image is responsibility, responsibility to care for the whole earth with a love that "images" God's love for the creation.²⁵

3. God's love of nature is evident in various biblical passages. Paul Santmire points to several notable ones: "Thus we hear that Yahweh knows the birds of the air (Ps. 50:1), that He calls the stars by name (Isa. 40:26), that both animals and humans are in His care (Ps. 36:5), and that He feeds them all (Ps. 145:14). Yahweh commands Noah to take the animals with him, two by two, in order to keep them alive (Gen. 6:19) and,

after the deluge, He makes his covenant with 'all the birds and animals' (Gen. 9:10) as well as with Noah and his descendants."[26] In addition to these, Santmire notes, one of the richest expressions of the beauty of creation and God's intimate involvement with it is to be found in Psalm 104.

4. Most important of all, creation and redemption are not separate matters in biblical faith. Redemption is not the ultimate hope of human beings alone, with the rest of creation being merely a temporary stage on which to play out the drama of human salvation. Rather, Jesus' resurrection victory is a victory for the redemption of the whole person and the whole world. It is a declaration and assurance of the coming reign of God in which *all things* will be new and whole (Rom. 8:19-21; 11:36; 1 Cor. 8:6; 15:22-28; Col. 1:15-20, for example). United with all things in being created by God, we are united with all things in being redeemed by God.[27]

These few biblical perspectives provide us with a vision of the final good of all creation, a vision that provides the basis for the intrinsic value of all of creation and, therefore, a strong and important resource for environmental ethics.

The ultimate good we discern in God's promise of creation and redemption might simply be stated in this way: *the viability and integrity of all creation.* To speak of viability is, of course, to speak of the triumph of life over death, decay, and destruction for all individuals in the human family and for all species of creation. In terms of the nonliving world, it is to speak of its ongoing ability to sustain life by providing a habitat in which life can thrive.

To speak of integrity is to speak of being intact, whole, healthy, or integrated. When sin divides us within ourselves and from one another, our integrity as whole individuals and our integrity as persons created for community is destroyed. Similarly, the reality of sin is experienced in the loss of integrity in our relationship with creation, a loss that threatens the integrity of nature itself. When humans threaten the extinction of species, destroy ecological systems, or cause the unnecessary suffering of animals, they are violating nature's integrity by degrading its intactness. Again, the cosmic scope of God's redeeming love communicates a promise for the new creation, revealed in Christ, that overcomes the forces that divide and threaten the integrity of all things.

Christian advocacy for the viability and integrity of the whole creation is a means to the fulfillment of our vocation, for commitment to creation's wholeness reflects our faith in the promise of God. That advocacy is further served when ethical norms, which correlate with our vision of the good and express the basic impulses of the Christian ethic, can be articulated as bases for strategic environmental decisions, corporate policy, and public policy.

AN ETHIC OF NORMS

Our understanding of the good further helps us to understand that human well-being and the well-being of the rest of creation are inextricably bound together in an organic unity in which both possess intrinsic value.[28] Therefore, our norms will need to concern both our responsibilities to one another and our responsibilities to the rest of creation. Obviously, this orientation goes beyond what many in business would intend by their embrace of "sustainable development." However, it is equally obvious that it is a moral vision compatible with the notion of sustainable development and one that adds depth to that notion.

As love seeks wholeness or the renewal of integrity in relationships among persons and wholeness and life for all persons, so it seeks to safeguard the integrity of nature in the wholeness of its myriad and complex ecosystems and protect and promote the viability of all its species.

This commitment of Christian love with respect to the environment can be spelled out somewhat further in certain specific norms. In fact, several of the norms that follow may be found in a number of church-related documents concerning environmental ethics.

1.Sustainability. The norm of sustainability commits us to practices and policies that enable natural resources and life support systems to be maintained indefinitely for a healthy and stable environment in which all living things can flourish.

We have, of course, already encountered the norm of sustainability in our discussion of sustainable development. The Presbyterian Church (USA), in its definition of *sustainability,* offers a statement that encompasses what is meant by sustainable development: "Sustainability is the capacity of the natural order and the socioeconomic order to thrive together."[29]

The concept of sustainability directs our concern toward safeguarding the self-renewing capacity of natural systems and toward reducing our reliance on nonrenewable resources. Earlier in this chapter we noted that this emphasis is a key component in achieving resource security, which, in turn, is one of three keys to sustainable development, according to the report of the National Wildlife Federation's Corporate Conservation Council.

Sustainability as an idea and an obligation evokes a mind-set of care for the earth that embodies some of the self-giving features of agape in its readiness to set aside certain immediate gratifications in concern for the long-term well-being of the creation and the neighbor in creation.

In the strategy and practice of business, this means a shift away from short-term profit to long-term thinking. In writing for the Business

Council for Sustainable Development, Stephen Schmidheiny refers to this as the "challenge of time." The challenge is for those who have benefited from past practices to give up some of that benefit for the sake of the long-term good of future generations. Says Schmidheiny:

> This is the crux of the problem of sustainable development, and perhaps the main reason why there has been great acceptance of it in principle, but less concrete actions to put it into practice: Many of those with the power to affect the necessary changes have the least motivation to alter the status quo that gave them that power.... But given that sustainable development requires a practical concern for the needs of people in the future, then it does ultimately require a new shared vision and a collective ethic based on equality of opportunity, not only among people and nations, but also between this generation and those to come.[30]

Once again, the particular contribution of Christianity is not better environmental strategies or novel ways of stating ethical principles for environmentalism, but a vision and a passion in which to ground the sort of ethic Schmidheiny sees as needed.

2. Justice through Sufficiency, Participation, and Solidarity. The Bible does not provide us with a theory of justice in terms of an abstract set of principles that govern public policy and social relations to guarantee fairness in all aspects of life. However, it does provide us with at least two strong clues as to how we must perceive justice and what just actions and policies will entail.

The first of these clues is that the Bible clearly links justice to mercy by lifting up God's compassion for the poor and by highlighting God's concern that people be freed from the bondages that afflict them. These emphases are throughout Scripture, but probably come to their ultimate expression and summation at the beginning of Jesus' public ministry, when he chose to interpret that ministry and its meaning by quoting the prophet Isaiah: "The Spirit of the Lord is upon me, because he has anointed me to bring good news to the poor. He has sent me to proclaim release to the captives and recovery of sight to the blind, to let the oppressed go free, to proclaim the year of the Lord's favor" (Luke 4:18-19). Justice as connected to mercy is concerned that basic needs be met and freedom assured.

Our second clue comes from the Sermon on the Mount, where Jesus teaches us, "Love your enemies and pray for those who persecute you, so that you may be children of your Father in heaven; for he makes his sun rise on the evil and on the good, and sends rain on the righteous and on the unrighteous" (Matt. 5:44-45). God's love and the love we are called to show exclude no one, not even our enemies. All are equally the concern of love. Thus, a justice born of the neighbor love which Jesus taught and exemplified will strive for equality.

With this orientation to justice as grounded in the biblical witness of mercy and love, it is possible to explicate the norm of justice in specifically environmental terms.

a. Sufficiency. In concert with God's mercy and with love's demand for equality, sufficiency highlights the dimension of justice that requires that we exercise stewardship of the world's natural resources in such a way that all peoples of the world have sufficient food, energy, and other needful goods to sustain a healthy and fulfilling life.

A serious commitment to sufficiency means a rethinking of values among the affluent toward lifestyles more geared to what is needful than to what is desired or possible. It involves a redress of the current situation in which the majority of the world's population does not enjoy sufficiency. In that connection, we need also to recognize the degradation of the environment not only violates the integrity of the creation but also has its greatest impact on the poor whose means are already insufficient.

The nuances of sufficiency are various, but it boils down to restraint in the face of greedy impulses that most all of us feel. There are a multitude of analogues in the world of business. William Diehl counsels Christians to perform a "ministry of lifestyle" by countering the preoccupation of many in business with status symbols and adopting, as a contrasting statement, a modest standard of living that is "just enough."[31] In our previous chapter we sampled Suzanne Gordon's feminist critique of our contemporary workplace culture in which she asserts that the drive for personal gain has become so dominant that it crowds out caring and the building of community. Adherence to the norm of sufficiency is a building block of justice and a true expression of love by the manner in which it gives of itself to meet the needs of others in the interest of community.

At the level of corporate commitment and concern for the environment, sufficiency could well be translated into a corporate willingness to forgo excessive short-term profits in order to make long-term investments in environmentally friendly technology transfer and development in less developed countries, a bold commitment that is good for the environment and good for the world community.[32]

b. Participation. To have the true freedom and equality that justice demands, participation is necessary. Participation in terms of our present concerns means enabling people everywhere to have a part in choosing those courses of action for the responsible use of natural resources that immediately affect their well-being. In a world characterized by a huge gap between the haves and the have-nots, the latter lack the economic and political power to participate in those decisions. Not only are they denied the sufficiency demanded by equality but also they are denied the freedom to act meaningfully for change. Ironically, our tradition of emphasizing personal freedom to seek whatever goods we desire has served to frustrate global participation by concentrating the wealth, resources, and power in the hands of relatively few, both within nations and societies and among nations and societies. The unbridled exercise of individual freedom or the unchecked freedom of individual societies to pursue their desires at the expense of the environment and the well-being of others needs to be tempered by the freedom and equality sought through participation.

Beyond this obvious need to foster participation for previously excluded populations, there is a need for the rest of creation itself to have a voice in the decisions we make that affect its destiny. That is certainly an implication of our conviction that the whole of creation is endowed with intrinsic value by the Creator. Those who speak for the nonhuman world in which we all participate need to have a voice of participation as well.

The growing recognition by groups like the Business Council for Sustainable Development and the National Wildlife Federation's Corporate Conservation Council that environmentalism and global economic justice are intimately linked as emerging obligations of international business, is a helpful step in the right direction.

More and more, companies and industries are recognizing the need to form partnerships and patterns of collaboration with communities and groups that were once their opponents in public debate but are now clearly among their stakeholders. An example of this is the Chemical Manufacturers Association initiative, Responsible Care,® which establishes six codes of management practice designed to ensure that corporations in the chemicals industry will exercise optimum responsibility for the environment. However, the key point here is that integral to the design and implementation of compliance with these codes are regular communication and dialogue with the communities affected and with people who represent interests outside the industry itself, including interests of environmentalism.[33]

c. Solidarity. The notion of solidarity overlaps in content the previous norm of participation. However, it has its own edge of meaning. Solidarity recognizes the organic interdependence and unity of the whole creation as the one work of the one God who loves it and redeems it. It calls upon us to act in modes of behavior and according to policies that uphold and sustain that community of creation.

From the standpoint of environmental ethics in business, solidarity as a principle directs our attention away from the idea that business can run on its own track with its only destination being the maximization of profit. Solidarity suggests, instead, that environmental costs and decisions of environmental responsibility must be integral to the general cost-benefit analysis of the business and the general decision making involved in day-to-day management. The integration of environmentalism and its implications for social justice into the corporate structure of policy formation and decision making is an essential step toward maximizing environmental responsibility as a concomitant of fiscal responsibility.[34]

In this chapter we have been able to focus on only a few points of contact for the dialogue of faith and work in quest of an environmental ethic. Much more needs to be done to make the connections. Specific strategic, technological, and regulatory initiatives need to be tested in dialogue with the imperatives of environmental ethics. Asserting the intrinsic value of all the natural world is an important step in building strong foundations for environmental ethics, but in our decision making we still need to determine the relative value of various entities. That all entities have intrinsic value does not mean that they have equal value. So, for example, how do we balance ensuring survival of the spotted owl and preserving old-growth forests in the Northwest with the economic and human costs exacted by those efforts? That things have intrinsic value does not mean that they do not also have instrumental value, perhaps in greater proportion.

The norms we have discussed also lend themselves to being understood as virtues. Theologian-ethicist James A. Nash mentions nine "ecological virtues" that include sustainability, sufficiency, and solidarity along with other familiar traits of character such as humility and frugality.[35] These ecological virtues have the same deep resonance in Christian thought as the norms they echo. Our previous discussion of the importance of character in business leadership for the development of an ethically strong corporate culture is worth reiterating in this connection. Insofar as the church is a community in which virtue and character are shaped and nurtured, the connections between Christian virtues and "ecological virtues" can be made, and Christians in business can be, correspondingly, better equipped to exercise leadership and contribute to a corporate culture of environmental responsibility.

As we aspire to this formidable vocation, we can take encouragement from the following statement from the 1990 document "Preserving and Cherishing the Earth: An Appeal for Joint Commitment in Science and Religion," by Carl Sagan, Hans Bethe, S. Chandrasekhar, and other prominent scientists: "We understand that what is regarded as sacred is more likely to be treated with care and respect. Our planetary home should be so regarded. Efforts to safeguard and cherish the environment need to be infused with a vision of the sacred.... There is a vital role for both religion and science."[36]

9

BEYOND CERTAINTY

One would think that the notion of moving beyond certainty is a bad fit with previous chapters, in which the "beyond" we were seeking in each case was presented as an attempt to move beyond an ethically less adequate approach to something ethically more adequate. Moving beyond certainty in ethics would seem to be an undesirable course, maybe even nonsensical. However, undue confidence of moral certainty in matters of ethical decision is often problematic.

In chapter 1 I observed that one of the factors contributing to the lack of dialogue between the church and the business world is the mistaken idea that "Christian" ethics really boils down to a few commonly held and perfectly clear rules of conduct. When persons also believe that the application of these rules is equally clear—and they often do believe this —the conclusion is easily reached that probing dialogue about ethics is really not needed; we simply need to weed out the unethical people!

Not long ago at a luncheon discussion of business ethics, I heard an executive from a nationally known company make a remark that is pertinent here. He observed that, while many CEOs firmly believe that good ethics is good business and believe that they practice that conviction, the way their organization is structured and the expectations they impose upon their managers show that they really do not grasp what "good ethics" involve—a more comprehensive reform of the corporate culture than usually happens.

Inadequate discernment of the complexity, difficulty, and ambiguity of many ethical decisions can lead to an unwarranted certainty and overconfidence in our judgments. This not only gets in the way of dialogue but also can produce an almost arrogant rigidity. More important, a byproduct of ethical overconfidence is often a lack of sensitivity in understanding the situation at issue and the needs of the people involved.

However, if, like many others, some businesspeople tend to oversimplify ethical issues and be overconfident, plenty in business recognize that ethics are often a struggle, and some of these people feel that ethicists have not always met their needs in this regard. In a 1993 *Harvard Business Review* piece, Andrew Stark, a professor of management, laments that much of what is taught in business ethics courses and textbooks is not sufficiently attuned to the complex and ambiguous decisions business leaders face. Ethicists deal too much with simple right versus wrong issues and not enough with difficult gray area situations and problem areas where competitive and institutional pressures undermine one's best intentions.[1] Whether or not Stark is correct in his indictment of business ethicists, it is clear that there is a widespread belief that ethical reflection in business must be prepared to deal with the tough cases.

Of course, all moral matters are not terribly complicated; many ethical decisions are straightforward and clear. Still others are fairly clear to most but have consequences that are hard to swallow. One executive I spoke with told of how it occasionally happened that a batch of a certain food product they manufactured would not be up to standards, even though it would still pass government inspection. For him, he said, the decision was easy; you take your loss and dump the batch rather than break faith with your consumers on the quality of the product.

Not all executives find themselves ready or think themselves able to take a loss or a risk of loss for the sake of a clear ethical requirement. Sometimes internal and external pressures seem so severe that doing the right thing seems impossible. Yielding to pressure in these situations is what Laura Nash has called a case of "acute rationalization," a situation in which even the best intentions and values are "melted down" by the heat of the dilemma.[2] In some instances this may be a real failure in ethical resolve, but in other cases it may be the sign of a real conflict-ridden dilemma in which doing the right thing seems impossible, and, whatever your choice, the outcome is uncertain and morally ambiguous.

Finally, to complete this brief account of uncertainty (and temptation) in ethical decision, some situations are simply hard to figure out. First of all, there are times when we are not sure if our actions or those of others are unethical. When does the enthusiastic portrayal of a product cease to be good promotion of a good product and start to become deceptive or manipulative? How far is it ethical to go in giving gifts or doing favors before it becomes a subtle form of bribery? How responsible are companies when people are harmed by the misuse of their product? If they have some responsibility, even if the misuse is not their fault, how does this recognition affect their marketing of the product?

Second, there are those situations when we feel a genuine sense of obligation to the needs of others but are not sure how to fulfill that need. A manager may be convinced that it is a moral duty to help those who work for her or him to achieve their best and get ahead in the company; what kinds of managerial style can best serve that end? When do you get tough? When is it better to be encouraging rather than critical, understanding rather than demanding? How do you separate your personal response to an employee's personal crisis from your supervisory responsibilities, or do you? How far is it appropriate to go in responding to the employee's personal needs if you do sense an obligation to do so?

Christians have a keen understanding of ambiguity in the moral life. In a fallen world in which sin has rendered things dysfunctional, we can expect uncertainty to be a fact of life. We know that the best of us remain sinners and that the old person within us is always locked in battle with the new person in Christ. Conflicting motives at work within us cloud our judgment as we try to discern what is right. They rob us of certainty about the virtue of our choices once we have made them. We know too that, while God's ideals of the good and the right are absolute, our abilities are finite. Not only are we sinners but also we are limited in what we can understand and do.

Of course, the problem of uncertainty is not only within. The world in which we live is equally imperfect. It presents us with choices that are often ambiguous and conflicting choices that are sometimes tragic. Most sensitive souls who have had to make decisions about downsizing a business in ways that affect persons and communities have agonized over these choices and felt caught up in a tragic dilemma beyond their power to control. Sometimes there are simply no good choices. Yet we are still responsible to choose and to live with that choice.

A case used in a business ethics program of the Presbyterian Church (USA) illustrates the kinds of agonizing dilemmas people often face. It is the story of Alice, a young supervisor who is being asked to cut back her staff by several people as part of a general downsizing in her company. The standard is to be seniority. Unfortunately, two of her workers with the least seniority are recently trained persons with disabilities who cannot shift to other jobs without significant retraining; they will be out in the cold. Seniority has been a long-established standard of justice in this corporation, but only recently have they come to realize that justice also demands that persons with disabilities receive training and opportunities to compete in the workplace. Thus, few persons with disabilities have any seniority in the company, and it seems impossible to honor the just claims of all individuals. Company traditions and cultural developments have combined to create a situation in a real sense beyond our control to resolve without harm to someone.[3]

In all of this ambiguity, Christians hear a word of judgment about the nature of our fallen world, but they also hear a word of grace. As children of God in Christ, we are set free from that judgment, not to do as we please! We are set free to struggle with the tough and tragic choices in the confidence of the gospel promise that God is with us to guide us and sustain us and affirm us. *The gospel promise is our certainty beyond certainty.* The idea that we can have total certainty in all our moral judgments, or even reasonable certainty, if it becomes the basis of our approach to ethics, leads to either complacency or despair.[4] Complacency is out of touch with the realism of Christian faith, which sees the fallen world for what it is. Despair is out of touch with the gospel promise. The certainty of the gospel promise does not eliminate the struggle of decision. But it does enable us to face that struggle with an appropriate blend of humility, confidence, and courage that comes with knowing you belong to Christ.

Within this framework of theological understanding, which is linked to the ideas on the life of Christian love in chapter 5, we can begin to explore a pattern of ethical decision making that is consistent with our Christian faith and understanding and yet suited to dialogue with ethical reflection outside the faith in the "secular" setting of business.

DIALOGICAL ETHICS

In my recent book *Faith, Formation, and Decision,* I discussed at some length the idea of dialogical ethics, a way of doing Christian ethics that I had introduced in earlier writings. We have been talking in this book about the dialogue between the Christian ethics and the ethics of business in a pluralistic world. The system of decision making that I am about to describe carries forward the same dynamics of dialogue that we have been discussing but, in this instance, the dialogue is between the rules or norms of Christian love and the situations of decision.

The conviction is that, in the openness of dialogue, the rules that describe the ethics of Christian love will illuminate the ethical issues in the situation confronting us, and the human situation of decision will, in turn, shed light on the meaning of love and how to apply it in that instance. This is a rather abstract proposition, but I hope the dynamics of dialogical decision making will become more concrete as we spell out the details of the system and attempt to illustrate its workings.

The General Rules of Love

The general rules of love are norms that define the obligations of love in various areas of life. It is important to emphasize that the general rules express *love.* The rules do not have a life of their own; they exist to serve the orientation of love's concern for the neighbor and the world. Thus, as love is a result of God's grace in Christ at work within us, so our embrace of love's rules is a further expression of that grace at work through love. Therefore, although the rules of love define obligations, they are not a set of legalistic demands; they are rather a set of directions for those who are free in Christ to give of themselves in uncoerced love. Because this is their status, we can speak of the general rules of love as "general" in two senses.

Universality. As love is the expression of God's will for humankind, the basis of all relationships, so the rules that define the conduct of love in those relationships are universally valid as expressions of God's sovereign will. Consequently, we go into situations with clear directions; despite the ambiguity we have discussed, some things are not in doubt. And in many situations of conflict where we are forced into terrible choices, the norms of love spell out just what has been sacrificed or compromised.

Generality. Because they give directions for uncoerced love rather than demands for the fulfillment of a legalistic moral code, the general rules of love can operate on the basis of generality. Since it is the neighbor's well-being and not the fulfillment of the rules that is the purpose of the rules, one can be open to interpreting the guidance of the rules in terms of the needs to be met in the situation. There is no need to elaborate on the demands of the rules by creating further rules and rules to cover exceptions to the rules because love serves the neighbor, not the rules, and the rules serve love. There is no need to develop more rules to delineate all the specific applications of the general rules in order to determine with certainty that we have done *the* right thing. Such certainty is illusory, as we have shown. Our certainty is neither in the adequacy of our rules to prescribe for all decisions nor the perfection of our obedience to them. Our certainty is in the promise of the gospel that sets us free to struggle with decision in the dialogue with human need.

As in my previous work, I am basing my statement of love's general rules on the content of the Ten Commandments. While I have used the language of public ethical discourse in naming those rules rather than simply repeating the biblical formulas, I have tried to remain faithful to the substance of the Decalogue as revealed in the biblical traditions and as interpreted in the history of Christian moral thought. These, then, are the general rules of love:

Respect for Autonomy. To respect the autonomy of other persons is to recognize their essential dignity as persons created in the image of God who are endowed with freedom and responsibility.[5] The kind of covenantal leadership and organization we saw Laura Nash describe—in which persons have the opportunity to be their best, make choices, and take responsibilities—supports autonomy. Paternalistic, hierarchical modes of management that seek maximum control, limit input, discourage personal initiative, and require conformity do little to foster respect for autonomy and may even force people to compromise their own integrity for job security.

Justice. Justice is related to respect for autonomy insofar as it refers to guaranteeing the freedom and equality of all persons. Justice also has to do with fairness in giving each person his or her due. We have already met issues of justice in our discussions of affirmative action and of how a biblically shaped concept of justice is served by the principles of sufficiency, participation, and solidarity in matters of environmental concern. Even the less global, day-to-day issues of justice in the workplace give rise to some very basic but challenging questions. Are procedures for evaluation and reward consistent and fair? Does the organizational structure allow employees a voice in matters that affect them most?[6]

Sanctity of Life. To protect, preserve, and enhance life means, of course, more than refraining from taking life. Love's commitment to the sanctity of life is a commitment to the well-being of the whole person that intersects with business concerns at a number of points. It is obvious that issues of environmental degradation, hazardous waste disposal, employee safety, and product liability have positive or negative impacts on well-being, depending on how they are handled. Equally important, although perhaps less obvious, is to inquire about the obligations of business to support agencies in their communities who are working to meet basic human needs.

Truth Telling. There is perhaps no vaster an arena of ethical concerns in business than those that arise in connection with honesty and truthfulness, in for example, advertising, describing a product, filing reports, reporting wrongdoing, giving appropriate credit, and owning up to mistakes. Dishonesty in pursuit of profit or promotion or protection is one of the constant temptations of business life.

Promise Keeping. Like telling the truth, keeping one's promises is at the heart of creating trustworthy, reliable business relationships. So fundamental is this principle that we hardly need to document how breaking promises shatters the healthy and harmonious relationships that are the focus of ethics. It is interesting to recall again that Laura Nash's covenantal ethics are geared to building a corporate philosophy of keeping promises to all stakeholders. In that ethical vision, relationships are more important than rules, and value delivered to all concerned is more important than the bottom line alone.

As stated earlier, these general rules of love derive from the Ten Commandments. Interestingly enough, business ethicist Michael Rion lists four of these five as the most commonly involved principles in business ethics decisions: fairness (we have said justice), honesty and honest communication (we have said truth telling), keeping promises, and doing no harm (we have said to protect the sanctity of life).[7] Once again, there is fertile ground for Christian, biblical categories and insights to connect in dialogue with more generally held beliefs.

The Dialogue of Decision

In dialogical ethics, decision is an outcome of dialogue between the general rules, which give us the shape of love's commitments, and the particular features of the situation calling for decision. I think of this dialogue as having three different forms, although the three types of dialogue may overlap with each other and often do.

1. Direct Interpretation. Sometimes when we enter upon an ethical decision, we think we know what norms are involved but are not sure how they apply in concrete terms. Sometimes we are not sure what kind of ethical problem we have and, therefore, what rules to apply and how.

In either case, we try to see how the norms of love shed light on the kind of ethical issues at stake, how the situation itself illuminates our obligations in love, and how we might specifically respond in love. "Direct interpretation" is this dialogical process.

Interpreting the situation to which we must respond is, first of all, getting clear on the facts. In some cases this can be very complicated indeed. Certainly a number of environmental concerns require extensive scientific analysis before there can be any recommended action that we would consider a moral obligation. Concerns for product safety in the manufacture and use of chemicals and drugs pose similar challenges at times. However, even if it is a relatively simple personnel matter, solid facts are still necessary for good ethical discernment.

A step beyond ascertaining the facts is to ask, "What's going on?" That is, what are the motives, expectations, felt needs, and real intentions of all the involved parties, including oneself? An appropriate response is impossible without knowing, as much as possible, what is going on with the people involved. Thus, for example, an astute manager will not make an important ethical decision concerning a plant or office operation in another location, home or abroad, without going there or sending a trusted aide for face to face meetings. In just the same way, an ethically astute person will want to come face-to-face with her or his own motives for any contemplated action.

Of course, direct interpretation frequently involves both a considerable amount of fact-finding and a considerable amount of discerning "what's going on." Issues of sexual harassment, in its manifold forms, certainly require reliable facts and the most sensitive kind of discernment for a satisfactory ethical response.

A number of ethicists working on issues in business find this kind of interpretive dialogue helpful in decision making. Michael Rion lists six questions to ask in dealing with ethical challenges. They reflect a similar quest for greater clarity on facts, motives, expectations, and needs in the interest of greater ethical clarity:

(a) Why is this bothering me? (What kind of ethical problem is this? Conflict? Ambiguity?)
(b) Who else matters? (Who has a stake in this matter, and what is it?)
(c) Is it my problem? (Do I go beyond the moral minimum? What can I really do?)
(d) What is the ethical concern? (Can we identify the norms that apply and how they apply?)
(e) What do others think? (What's going on?)
(f) Am I being true to myself? (Check motives and consult conscience.)[8]

Laura Nash has extensive lists of questions, often framed in specifically business-related terms, designed to foster interpretive dialogue: "Am I perpetuating a dishonest or fraudulent relationship?" "How will this decision affect our customers' trust in us?"[9] She also has more general, probing questions to test our own motives and moral sensitivity as we carry out the dialogue and contemplate certain decisions: "Could I disclose this to the public or a respected mentor?" and "Would I tell my child to do this?" to give two examples.[10]

2. Conflict Resolution. Frequently, the dialogue of decision focuses on the resolution of conflict. Obligations to two or more different rules of love involved in a situation seem to be in conflict, or the claims of two or more parties affected by a decision seem to be in conflict with each other.

The case of Alice, previously described, is a case of conflicting obligations under what are conceivably two different rules. On the one hand, the traditional standard of seniority in determining layoffs is a promise that has been made to all employees. On the other hand, genuine equal opportunity for the disabled through training, accommodation, and affirmative action is an obligation under justice.

In other cases a variety of "stakeholders" have a "stake" in the decisions a company makes, including employees, stockholders, suppliers, customers, and the community. The company's management feels an obligation to be concerned for the needs of all stakeholders but may at times find that the claims of one or more of the stakeholders are in conflict with those of others.

Most of the cases used for discussion of ethical decision making in business and in other fields are cases that involve conflict resolution. They reflect some of the most difficult dilemmas we encounter in real life. There is a need for some guidance as we steer our way through the conflict-resolution process. I have found it helpful to operate with a set of axioms that can help us clarify and make our choices in resolving conflict, although they by no means prescribe those choices.[11]

Distinguish between Interest and Need. Sometimes it is possible to determine that the claims of one or more parties in a conflict are *interests* rather than needs. Since needs are of greater moral significance than interests, we act in favor of those with needs. In a product safety case, for example, the legitimate interests of the company for profitability are sometimes in conflict with the potential needs of the customer who may suffer harm from unsafe products. Hard as it may be to bite the bullet, the interests of the company must take a back seat to the needs of the customer by taking the product off the market, correcting the problem, and absorbing the short-term losses.

Limitation or Modification. Sometimes conflicts can be dealt with by partially meeting the needs of all concerned by limiting or modifying our response to their claims upon us. This is the world of trade-offs or compromise, as in the agreements reached in labor-management negotiations. In our case of Alice and the two persons with disabilities on her staff, some modification of company policy might be envisioned that could still be fair to the great majority of those with seniority while responding to the needs of workers with disabilities. For example, if seniority were looked at on a companywide basis instead of department by department, Alice's handicapped workers might have enough time in to be spared. At the same time, a new policy might be developed, with employee input, to give separate consideration to specially trained persons with disabilities who have limited mobility in the job market and in whom the company has a serious investment.

The Gradation of Higher and Lower Needs or Values. Sometimes it is possible to favor one obligation over another because the need involved is the greater need. The head of a small company told me recently how he discovered a cooperative health plan that would be less costly and, therefore, enable him to pay a higher wage from the savings. However, he soon discovered that workers who lived in two adjacent states would not receive equal coverage in the new plan due to the difference in their states' regulation of health care cooperatives. In weighing the relative needs and values involved, he came to the conclusion that uniform health benefits in the interest of justice and employee well-being were a higher need or value than savings to the company and higher wages.

Consequently, he went to a more expensive plan that was able to deliver uniform coverage for all employees.

In his development of an environmental ethic, James Nash has argued that nonhuman creatures should have a bill of "biotic rights." However, he also recognizes a hierarchy of relative value among various forms of life. Thus, the genuine, morally valid needs of human beings may on occasion justifiably override the needs of other creatures who are lower in the hierarchy of value.[12] Nash's recognition of a hierarchy among living things, who nonetheless all have rights, provides a good example of how the gradation of values we find in a conflict situation can sometimes provide the key to resolving that conflict.

Inclusiveness. On occasion it is possible to resolve a conflict by deciding to honor the obligation that appears to benefit the most people. When corporations downsize by closing plants and terminating jobs, there may be some stopgap measures that can soften the blow, such as job retraining, outplacement services, and compensation to the community. However, the inescapably difficult decision that some will inevitably have to suffer in the process of company survival may be made on the basis of inclusiveness; some will lose out, but the greatest number will gain if the organization remains solvent and profitable.

No matter how useful the axioms may be and no matter how solid our reasoning, resolution of conflict mostly ranges from difficult to agonizing and tragic. Our decision may be the most responsible one possible, but we also recognize that harm could not be avoided and the unalloyed good could not be done. The Christian witness is that God's promise in Christ gives strength for bold decision in a flawed, conflicted, and often tragic existence.

3. The Formation of Middle Axioms. When the dialogue between the general rules of love and the situation deals with not simply one incident but a whole area of moral concern, the result is usually the formation of middle axioms. Middle axioms give a more specific statement of a general rule obligation as it is interpreted and applied in a particular area of ethical focus. Thus, church bodies in issuing social statements on crucial issues such as environmental responsibility, economic justice, or fair housing practices normally formulate middle axioms that give more specific guidance on these issues than the general rules, such as justice and respect for autonomy, on which they are based. These more specific guidelines do not prescribe decision; they are in the middle between general rules and specific decisions or policy directions.

Codes of ethics for businesses, professional organizations, or industry organizations are often a collection of middle axioms that tailor the implications of general principles to the specifics of the organization.

The American Society of Chartered Life Underwriters and Chartered Financial Consultants has a code of ethics for its members that affirms two general imperatives: to serve the client and engender public trust. However, the guides to interpreting and acting on these general principles are a more elaborate set of middle axioms that enjoin such obligations as resolving conflicts of interest in favor of the client, providing accurate information, not misleading the customer for the sake of a sale, and keeping clients informed of all developments that could affect their well-being.[13]

United Technologies Corporation has organized their company credo in terms of the basic relationships that characterize their corporate life: customers, employees, suppliers, shareowners, competitors, and communities. For each of these relationships, the credo spells out how fundamental obligations of justice, respect for persons, honesty, promise keeping, and other matters apply. This application of basic principles to the sorts of interaction involved in these different relationships is a good example of formulating middle axioms. The description of commitment to employees should suffice as an example:

> We are committed to treating one another fairly, and to maintaining employment practices based on equal opportunity for all employees. We will respect each other's privacy and treat each other with dignity and respect irrespective of race, color, sex, religion or nationality. We are committed to providing safe and healthy working conditions and an atmosphere of open communication for all our employees.[14]

Middle axioms can be more specific, but this example does illustrate going one step beyond the most general of rules. Thus, the obligation to respect the sanctity of life is framed in terms of safe and healthy work conditions. More dialogue will then be needed to determine the specific actions entailed.

Whether the dialogue of decision is a direct interpretation of how to apply a general rule of love, the resolution of conflict, or the development of middle axioms and the dialogical process of applying them, we recognize that the process of decision is responsible but not foolproof. Once again, we are not blessed with certainty; we are blessed with assurance. To draw this theme out and further sample the workings of dialogical decision making, we turn to a common problem area for ethics in business.

BLOWING THE WHISTLE: TRUTH TELLING AND CONFLICT

In January of 1992 the *Columbus Dispatch* ran a Sunday feature on "whistle-blowers," persons in government and business who exposed wrongdoing within their organizations. Examples of the things they blew the whistle on were cover-up of a radioactive spill, brutality by a hospital security official, and falsified cost reports. In addition, the article featured a whistle-blowers hall of fame with such famous names as Karen Silkwood and Frank Serpico, as well as the well-known case of Roger Boisjoly's repeated warnings about the O-rings on the ill-fated space shuttle Challenger. What all the less-known and better-known whistle-blowers appear to have in common is that they paid a heavy price for being truthful.[15]

In a companion article, "Poor Health Is Often the Price of Courage," a variety of researchers indicate that, while whistle-blowing is on the upswing and certainly more publicized, these ethically troubled truth tellers still suffer materially, socially, and emotionally. One researcher found that "whistleblowers frequently suffer from depression, stress and anxiety. Some develop allergies, others get divorced, and about 10 percent turn suicidal. Many go to an early grave."[16]

People who discover what they are certain is wrongdoing in the workplace almost always find themselves in the middle of a conflict. Telling the truth might jeopardize job security and, with it, family well-being. As we have seen, physical and emotional health could well be at risk. In some cases disclosure may threaten the health of the organization and with it the welfare of co-workers and other stakeholders. At the same time, honoring conscience and truthfulness may serve to protect investors or safeguard the lives of consumers.

It is not hard to see how the axioms for resolving conflict that I described previously could be of some use in sorting out the choices facing whistle-blowers. In matters of faulty production or the leakage of hazardous materials, where life and limb are at stake if the truth is not told, those in possession of that truth might be led to tell it because, despite risk to self, protecting life from harm is a higher value than protecting self and others from potential financial loss. However, in some instances a person may decide that the discovery is not serious enough to visit trouble upon one's family and co-workers. In this case, the reasoning may be that overlooking the discovery of wrongdoing will benefit the most and truth will be compromised for the most inclusive choice. Other examples using other axioms could easily be constructed.

While it is not hard to see the axioms we have looked at being helpful to some extent, it is also not hard to see that using such axioms to work through conflict will not eliminate the element of compromise. In conflict situations such as those faced by many whistle-blowers, something of the good is inevitably sacrificed. Loyalty to co-workers and company may suffer for the sake of the truth. The truth may suffer and illicit practices may go unpunished for the sake of a greater good or a greater number of needs. For the sake of protecting the public from harm a family may lose its breadwinner and a spouse his or her partner to emotional breakdown.

For Christians the decisional dynamics and the probable consequences of whistle-blowing decisions are no different from those faced by non-Christians. Certainly in the freedom of the gospel there is courage to act, but the specific course of action for which one must take courage is not prescribed. And, as we have been saying, once the courage to act has been summoned, the choice of action is no more clothed in certainty for Christians than it is for non-Christians. Beyond certainty there is only the promise of God's acceptance and the assurance of that which we need to weather the storms of our most terrible choices.

However, as Christian love struggles with conflicts in its obligations, it is motivated to do more than just choose the lesser of evils. Christian love will want to go the extra mile and become proactive rather than just reactive about truth telling in the workplace. Ethics is about more than just making the "right" decision. It is, as we observed in an earlier chapter, also a matter of creating an environment in which the ethical commitments of each person are valued and people are respected for being true to those commitments. Let us explore this ethical concern for a moment, first by looking at a different outlook, an attitude hostile to the whistle-blower. Back in 1981 management guru Peter Drucker wrote the following: " 'Whistle-blowing,' after all, is simply another word for 'informing.' And perhaps it is not quite irrelevant that the only societies in Western history that encouraged informers were bloody and infamous tyrannies—Tiberius and Nero in Rome, the Inquisition in the Spain of Philip II, the French Terror, and Stalin.... For under 'whistle-blowing,' under the regime of the 'informer,' no mutual trust, no interdependencies, and no ethics are possible."[17]

Doubtless, many business and organizational leaders share Drucker's rather stunning condemnation of whistle-blowing. Fortunately, his remarks drew a significant critical response from the opposite viewpoint.[18] More important, many business leaders have taken a different view as well.

Businesses have increasingly become aware of the need to make truth telling less threatening and to regard it as more an asset than a liability. Hotlines for anonymous reporting, ombudsmen, special committees of the board, and other devices to ensure the immunity of the reporter from reprisals and guarantee an honest investigation are more and more being built into the structure of corporate life. It is here, too, that Christians can be in the vanguard of seeking those kinds of conditions in which truthfulness can flourish and harm be prevented as much as humanly possible. Then, too, structures and procedures are no better than the people who implement them and the motives that impel them. The Christian witness that truthfulness is an expression of love's concern for the well-being of those affected can add depth to understanding the value of truth. Its understanding of the agony of decision that so often afflicts the whistle-blower can help to develop some needed appreciation of these beleaguered folks.

EXPANDING THE DIALOGUE

A final note is in order about dialogical decision making. The decision-making dialogue between principles and situation can also benefit by being included in a dialogue among various parties associated with a decision. This is important in today's world of complex organizations and interrelationships.

In the April 1993 issue of the *Business Ethics Quarterly Review,* Michael G. Bowen and F. Clark Power use the case of the *Exxon Valdez* disaster as a vehicle for discussing what they term "communicative ethics," a dialogical approach to making ethical decisions. Decision makers enlist as many involved parties as possible to participate in the decision or decisions that must be made. Through sharing knowledge, expertise, insights, and differing perspectives, the chances of making the most responsible decision in multifaceted and conflictual situations are greatly improved.[19]

The authors point out that the events leading up to the spill had a lengthy and complicated development, involving a variety of parties: those who ran the pipeline project, the state of Alaska, the Coast Guard, Alaska's Department of Environmental Conservation, Exxon itself, and various levels of leadership in all these organizations. Over a considerable period of time, these various players were involved at one time or another with a variety of decisions leading up to the disaster and in response to it. At every step of the way there were conflicting claims, and the consequences of any given decision in sorting out those conflicts were usually uncertain. In view of this complex picture, it is simplistic to imagine that certain managers in this case had clear facts and clear moral directives and simply failed to do the right thing.[20]

In intricate and perplexing situations in which a number of stakeholders are influencing events and choices are ambiguous, the notion of a moral manager acting individually in accord with clear moral directives is unrealistic. The new model of moral management will not only bring norms into dialogue with the situation in the ways we have described but also include an open dialogue among the widest possible variety of those involved. The authors suggest that businesses should practice this process through establishing imaginary dialogue situations as a tool for teaching managers this communicative ethic.[21]

The Bowen and Power model for expanding the decisional dialogue to some extent pulls together our preceding discussion of dialogical ethics with our main contention that dialogue is an avenue for Christians to bring their witness to bear in shaping the ethical consensus of a diverse society. Their model is an attempt to help managers deal with the ethical dilemmas of complex and ambiguous situations. Our views on dialogue have thus far focused on Christian ethical vocation in a pluralistic world. Yet, despite these distinctions, there is a synergy between the two concerns because the response to each is to foster open dialogue among diverse parties.

It is time, then, to revisit some of our contentions about dialogue and to voice some needed caveats as to its limits.

10

BEYOND THE
COMPANY WALLS

When I was about eleven years old, I had an enormous crush on a beautiful little girl who lived nearby. I carried that torch all the way into my teens! One day, as I was playing near her house, my football accidentally rolled onto the newly seeded lawn that her father had just finished planting and rolling out. For a brief moment I considered dashing onto the lawn, grabbing the ball, and running like crazy, but I did not.

I left the ball lying there, walked home, and told my father what had happened. Dad walked me back to her home, and together we talked to her dad, who found the solution to the problem. He got a clothespole long enough to reach the ball and roll it off the lawn without anyone having to step on it. I said I was sorry that it happened. However, her father said that he was grateful to me for being so conscientious; most kids would have run onto the lawn without caring, he said. Later Dad told me he was proud of me.

Apparently I did the right thing, but the point is *not* to tell you what a good boy I was, which would be immodest and probably untrue. I want to reflect instead on what I learned about ethics from this experience.

I said it would be untrue to picture myself as morally precocious at age eleven because my motives were not all that lofty. First of all, I was doubtless anxious to stay on good terms with the family given my passionate feelings for their daughter. (That did no good, by the way; I never did succeed at winning her heart, only her friendship.) Second, I was also motivated by the fear of consequences, should I be caught doing the wrong thing. My erstwhile girlfriend's father was, it seemed to me, a stern and strict man. Getting caught wrecking his lawn in pursuit of my errant football was sure to have a terrible end. My behavior was not morally significant as a reflection of high-minded motives, but what I learned about ethics on that occasion was significant.

I can still remember how pleased this man was, not only that his lawn was spared but, I think, also that he had experienced consideration and kindness. His person had been respected and his needs cared about, even if only by a scared little boy whose footprints on his lawn would not have done great damage. Although I did not understand it at the time, there was something of great importance in this otherwise unremarkable incident. I had accidentally tapped into something that is deep in the human spirit, a need to regard and be regarded. To respect each other and each other's needs, no matter what their magnitude or seeming significance, is life-giving and at the heart of ethics in all its applications.

Despite the great diversity in our communities, our society, and our world, there is an innate appreciation of what ethics is all about, an appreciation that makes our differences intelligible and dialogue possible.

Certainly, there are strong currents of theological conviction that give doctrinal shape to our experiential encounter with the elemental moral impulses within the people we meet. In Romans 2 Paul writes that the Gentiles, who had not received the law through Moses, nonetheless did instinctively what the law requires (v. 14). "They show that what the law requires is written on their hearts, to which their own conscience also bears witness" (v.15). This Pauline perspective is echoed in later Christian sources, which attribute to humankind a natural understanding of God's law for our lives or speak instead of a "civil righteousness" that, despite the ravages of sin, is still a part of what we are. Civil righteousness reflects an innate ability to understand the ethical requirements for a just society that provides for the common good.[1]

Although the biblical and Christian doctrine of universal, original sin reminds us how fragmented and fragile our innate sense of the right and the good really is, the sense is still there. It provides the fertile ground of dialogue and mutual understanding. There is a basis for sharing various moral convictions in the true hope that we can understand and learn from each other in a mutual quest for a better state of affairs.

Christians need to be reminded, as noted ethicist Daniel Maguire suggests, of the enormous and lasting contribution the Christian witness has made to the ethical culture of our world. Christians took the biblical teaching of our creation in the divine image as evidence of the equality of all persons and asserted it in defiance of Roman totalitarianism. In so doing, they laid the foundations for the Western belief in freedom and the infinite worth of each individual. In numerous battles with oppressive forces, Judaism and Christianity stood for the dignity of every person, a stance echoed in today's bills of rights.[2]

We have encouragement, then, for the task of moral witness, encouragement in the discovery of an ineradicable moral core in the human

makeup, encouragement in the traditions of our faith, and encouragement in the historical impact of our witness.

There is even encouragement within the company walls for the kind
of intentional dialogical processes so necessary for self-conscious
Christian participation in shaping the ethics of business. We have already
seen a proposal for "communicative ethics," a form of dialogical decision
making that calls for interactive consultation among persons involved in
some of the more complex problems of corporate life. It is a proposal
that also calls for creating dialogue groups in which managers can hone
the skills of dialogical decision making.[3]

I have one more anecdotal example. A friend of mine does diversity
training for a sizeable company. Part of the process is to harness the
existing diversity of the company by placing persons of various backgrounds and various levels of responsibility together in dialogue groups.
Despite incorporating several dimensions of diversity, the groups have
the task of discovering a common ethical commitment to make diversity
work in the interests of justice and the common good of the corporate
community. The process is not without its problems, but it certainly
provides another hopeful model in and through which persons can follow their conscience and make a contribution.

There is some encouragement within the walls of the company. As
genuine dialogue about ethical issues becomes more and more a part of
workplace culture, the necessary avenues for Christian participation are
opened up.

Despite these encouragements, we cannot underestimate the difficulty
of the task. Many organizations are a long way from being open to the
kind of interaction we have been considering. As organizational leadership struggles to adjust to the need for a new approach, there is a need to
create voluntary structures for dialogue beyond the company walls that
enable representatives of different organizations to talk with one another
on ethical issues of common interest. Arrangements of this sort provide
for a free flow of ideas unhindered by the influences and pressures of
company politics and policies. What is needed is a relatively "safe" environment in which questioning can occur and in which new insights can
germinate and grow for transplanting *within* the corporate environment.

NEW COALITIONS FOR NEW INSIGHTS

In chapter 8, where we discussed environmental ethics, I cited the report
Changing Course, prepared by Stephen Schmidheiny and Lloyd
Timberlake for the Business Council for Sustainable Development. The
council is itself a new coalition, an international voluntary association of

business leaders organized to deal more effectively with the environmental challenge. The council in aggregate is able to make proposals and marshal data that its members might find hard to do on their own. This is one way in which the dialogue on ethics is taken beyond company walls to good effect.

However, Schmidheiny and his colleagues see a need for even more diverse collaborations:

> New forms of collaboration are needed, including focus groups, advisory panels, forums for dialogue, and joint ventures. Building stakeholder involvement in the context of sustainable development extends the idea of corporate responsibility in time and space. Companies now have to consider the effects of their actions on future generations and on people in other parts of the world. Prosperous companies in a sustainable world will be those that are better than their competitors at "adding value" for *all their stakeholders,* not just for customers and investors.[4]

This counsel puts one in mind of steps already taken by the Chemical Manufacturer's Association. As we noted in chapter 8, its Responsible Care® initiative, designed to maximize safety and environmental responsibility, has incorporated dialogue with community representatives and others outside the industry as an aid to planning and implementation of the initiative's goals. One such dialogue group, the Public Advisory Panel, brings together a variety of persons including environmental advocates, scientists, engineers, public servants, and at least one representative of religious ethics. The 1992-93 progress report on Responsible Care® describes the insights gained from a recent meeting of the advisory panel. Here is a salient excerpt:

> If systems and procedures and technical measurements are not enough to drive Responsible Care,® what else is needed? Two days of panel discussion and activity in Raleigh-Durham...suggest that honest dialogue—between industry and the public, and between plants and local communities—is a crucial element in bringing about the industry-wide cultural change required by Responsible Care®. Whether discussing the challenges of relating laboratory findings to the complexities of the human and natural world, the possibility of integrating specific areas of Responsible Care with the CERES Principles, or meeting with leading members of Southerners for Economic Justice, panel members demonstrated the value of bringing a real world, public perspective to the table. The panel process, as seen in this and previous meetings, is an example of the kind of dialogue that keeps industry from talking only to itself.[5]

It is tempting to dismiss this kind of account as another instance of business patting itself on the back for token efforts whose primary goal is, after all, good public relations. However, many observers from out-side the industry who are close to the Responsible Care® initiative believe it is for real.[6]

The examples given so far of dialogue outside the company walls are industry and interindustry coalitions with membership interaction and outreach to representatives of other involved groups and communities. There are other kinds of coalitions of a slightly different sort that deserve mention as well. Specifically, I have in mind the example of the Council for Ethics in Economics (CEE) based in Columbus, Ohio. At the end of chapter 4, I mentioned that the council began as an offshoot of the dia-logue with Ross Laboratories over the infant-formula controversy. Its development since that time some twelve years ago is instructive.

Through the efforts of Paul Minus, president of the council, a small, hardworking staff, and a group of dedicated volunteers, CEE has grown to an organization of significant size with organizational and individual memberships from the fields of business, the professions, religion, and higher education. It is the mission of the council to bring together lead-ers in these fields that they might work together "to strengthen the ethi-cal fabric of business and economic life."[7]

Always emphasizing and promoting the benefits of interdisciplinary dialogue, CEE has provided regular programming for business leaders, institutions of higher education, and congregations. This approach is nowhere more evident than in a major project on honesty involving workgroups representative of the whole spectrum of CEE's constituency and membership. It is largely as a result of these ongoing programs that valuable ethical insights have been gained for sharing with other busi-nesses through the council's consulting services.

As CEE recognized the benefits and necessity of interdisciplinary dia-logue in our complex society, it was brought to the additional conviction that such an approach was even more urgently needed in the pluralistic environment of emerging international business. Consequently, in 1992, after years of planning, CEE convened a highly successful international conference on the ethics of business in a global economy, which was attended by leaders of business, religion, and higher education from more than twenty different countries and six continents. As a result of this conference, a five-year follow-up plan on issues of international business is now under way.[8]

More could be reported about the work of CEE, but enough has been said to demonstrate its ability to grow and move forward with its work. This is a valuable message for our purposes because the council is an example of an organization devoted to ethics in business in which busi-nesspeople voluntarily and enthusiastically participate with leaders from religion. For this reason CEE provides a particularly important model from our vantage point, although all the new coalitions mentioned, and others not included, are important to the shaping and promotion of ethical business in today's world.

The participation of church leaders, as well as that of Christian businesspersons, in organizations like CEE reminds us that the churches have a role of their own to play in promoting dialogue. In a real sense we have already been discussing that role by discussing the vocation of Christians and their contributions to the ethics of business. However, at this point I want to shift the focus to the witness and activities of the church as an institution in the world rather than confining our understanding of the church's witness to the activities of individual members in their various institutions.

THE CHURCH IN GLOBAL DIALOGUE

It is time to recall the thesis offered by Hans Küng, which we touched upon in chapter 3. Küng believes that the world's religions must lead the way in formulating and promoting a global ethic that can address international issues of peace, the environment, and economic justice. Religion alone, Küng maintains, can provide the element of transcendence necessary to establish the authority of a global ethic that spans the incredible diversity of our pluralistic world.[9] Reason has been unable to provide a universal way to ethical consensus.[10]

Küng observes, as we have done earlier, that we live in a postmodern world that is multicultural and pluralistic. In this contemporary global environment, he argues, dialogue is required. The religions of the world will need to be in dialogue with each other if they are to share constructively in the task of providing a basis for a truly global ethic. That means a self-critical openness to the views of one's dialogue partners. Dogmatic rigidity does not work. Intolerance is impossible. The capacity for dialogue begins with respect for the worth of the partners' position. The capacity for dialogue is virtually identical to the capacity for peacemaking.[11]

At the same time that Küng commends openness, he also cautions that openness does not mean sacrificing the truth and convictions of one's own faith. It is possible to be open and self-critical and yet steadfast. To be constant and consistent and courageous in adherence to what one understands to be the vital center of one's tradition is not incompatible with dialogue.[12]

The goal of dialogue is not to convert your partners and emerge victorious; it is to seek that blend of common commitments that can be derived from a right understanding of one another's beliefs. Such common commitments may be facilitated when those holding different positions learn from one another and make some adjustments to their own views, but the expectation remains that all partners will preserve the fundamental integrity of their own doctrines.

If the church is to take part in the kind of dialogue Küng sees as essential, it may well be that Christian businesspeople will play a key role in encouraging and enabling the churches to embrace that challenge. As Christians in business are increasingly confronted with the ethical dilemmas of international business and environmental concerns, they develop their own expertise in understanding the problems and in beginning to map the intersections between those problems and the insights of their faith. They can now expand the scope of their vocation. To their calling as individual Christians who witness in business circles, they can add the calling of providing knowledgeable leadership for the church to be active in fostering ethics for a global economy and global harmony.

For most of our century the church's activities on behalf of global justice and peace have proceeded in dialogue with political structures. Now, with the expanding development of a global economy, attention to the ethics of international business is a key component in the pursuit of global justice and peace. Working in dialogue with business leaders worldwide to influence the development of international standards of ethical business is not optional, and concentrating efforts for justice on the government control of international business is unrealistic.

The church is an important partner and can even be a leader in the effort to establish global dialogue for global ethics. It possesses a number of characteristics that equip it well for that role:

• Like the international business community itself, the church and its members transcend national boundaries to constitute an international network with an international mission.

• The church is where the people are, at the grassroots, in their communities, intimately in touch with the realities of human need so inextricably tied to economic conditions shaped by global business.

• At its best the church exists for the benefit of all people rather than for its own self-interest. Even the most high-minded corporations, labor unions, industry groups, and the like cannot escape entirely the perspective of their own goals; that is what they exist to promote.

• The church is, or should be, free in the security of the gospel promise to model the kind of self-critical openness required for international, multicultural dialogue.

• The church has, as the mandate of its love ethic in witness to the coming reign of God, a call to promote reconciliation at all levels of life. Dialogue among parties in a pluralistic world fits in that portfolio.

The Limits of Dialogue:
Conscience and Confrontation

We have said a great deal about the openness required for dialogue and given some attention to the need to overcome dogmatic intransigence. However, we have also said, and should reiterate, that dialogue does not mean abandoning convictions and betraying conscience. While we may have to negotiate the best possible agreement on the ethical standards that will govern an organization or transactions between organizations through the give-and-take of dialogue, and while that agreement may be a compromise in some respects, our ethical standards as Christian people are not thereby compromised.

As we have learned from Hans Küng, through his discussion of "steadfast dialogue," the quest for consensus through dialogue does not mean that ethical standards are constantly up for grabs. Rather, it means that consensus building in a situation of diversity will simply reflect those points on which the parties involved can agree. Partners in this dialogue will individually stick to their convictions, even though they agree to settle for less in the ethos of the whole organization. Indeed, confrontation is often an ingredient in dialogue.

However, there are still times when dialogue is not possible, and direct confrontation is necessary before dialogue can begin. Earlier I recalled the dialogue I was a part of with Ross Laboratories concerning the infant formula controversy. That dialogical approach was also pursued by the United Methodist Church task force on infant formula concerns in their dealings with Nestlé and others in the industry.[13] However, I think it fair to say that neither of these church-industry dialogues would have been likely, had not other church groups first pursued a confrontational approach to what they considered to be an unresponsive industry. It was not until after the boycott against Nestlé was under way and efforts to mobilize international opinion against industry marketing in the Third World had gone forward that the first efforts at dialogue were begun.

We have also discussed the Chemical Manufacturer's Association development of Responsible Care,® with its admirable use of dialogue among stakeholders to build a more advanced and responsive ethos of safety and environmental responsibility. Yet here, too, even those in the industry admit that the public outcry over disasters like Bhopal, the challenges of the environmentalists, and a generally deteriorating public image for the chemical industry were confrontational forces that gave great impetus to the development of the Responsible Care® initiative.[14]

THE REAL AND THE REALLY REAL

The preceding remarks on the limits of dialogue and the demands of conscience and confrontation that do indeed arise, both inside and outside the dialogical process, remind us that our enthusiasm and encouragement are always balanced by demands of realism. That has, I think, been a recurrent pattern in this discussion.

This book is meant as an encouragement to Christians in the world of business: an encouragement to affirm their vocation of witness to the Christian hope through participation in the shaping of ethical business and an encouragement to dialogue as an effective avenue for that witness in our pluralistic world, one that can help bridge the shareability gap between faith and work both inside and outside the church.

At the same time that we offer encouragement, Christian realism calls on us to address constructively some profound concerns that could otherwise easily lead us into discouragement. Those concerns are located in the question of our modern culture. Can our American culture, which has shaped business and been shaped by business, provide the fertile soil for meaningful growth in standards and conduct of ethical business that benefit all the people? What are the contributions and threats of our emerging global economic culture to that possibility?

It is beyond our scope in this study to address the second question. We may not even be ready for it yet. However, in any case, it is sufficient for our purposes to focus on the first question, recognizing that the geographical boundaries of the observations that follow may not always be limited to American soil.

Ethicist Larry L. Rasmussen has done some social analysis in his assessment of the state of contemporary public morality. His conclusion is that the communities that were the breeding ground of our moral consensus have been undermined by the forces of modernity, and public morality has suffered commensurately:

> Whatever tally we take, the moral emergency we face is that the communities that have given lasting shape to the moral life and perduring substance to moral convictions, from intact families to intact schools and neighborhoods to intact towns and cities with intact ways of life that endure over time and have common memories and practices that anchor shared socialization, are largely gone. The acids of modernity have dissolved these, and the scattered postmodern soul has not restored them.[15]

The "acids of modernity" are the combined effect of a variety of factors in the evolution of the modern world that have contributed to this state of affairs. The market society that has fostered the growth of business and industry is only one contributor, but it is a contributor.

To paraphrase Rasmussen all too briefly, free-market capitalism started with the assumption that the public morality necessary to govern our free enterprise for the common good was in place. However, the ethos of free-market capitalism ended up becoming the public morality; that is, as the development of free-market capitalism increased, it gave birth to the kind of individualism and even egocentrism that undermined the communities where moral standards were generated and sustained. In place of those communities of moral vision and the moral vision itself, we were left with a mass society, organized by markets in which the philosophy of free-market capitalism becomes the new proxy for public morality.[16]

Certainly, as Rasmussen himself points out, free-market capitalism, as an institution of modernity, has produced morally significant gains in providing greater freedom and prosperity for more people. That is no small matter. However, if free-market capitalism is and remains a counterforce to the sort of sustained community needed for basic moral formation, does it make any sense to talk about the ethical formation of its progeny in the corporate world? Is that like throwing your seeds on rocky ground?

Writing from an African American perspective, Cornel West asks why we are witnessing a breakup of black civil society and its cultural institutions, the very institutions that historically sustained the African American community through the most trying times. In West's analysis, one of the two major reasons is the influence of what he calls "corporate market institutions," which are, if I understand him correctly, the businesses of our society and their allies. These institutions have, in West's judgment, created a culture of consumption in their unlimited drive for profits, a culture of consumption and economic gain that has intruded on every sphere of our society. Specifically, the aggressive marketing of *pleasure*—comfort, convenience, and sexual stimulation—has greatly undermined traditional morality, in general, and moral traditions in the black community, in particular.[17] He writes:

> Like all Americans, African Americans are influenced greatly by the images of comfort, convenience, machismo, femininity, violence, and sexual stimulation that bombard consumers. These seductive images contribute to the predominance of the market-inspired way of life over all others and thereby edge out nonmarket values—love, care, service to others—handed down by preceding generations. The predominance of this way of life among those living in poverty-ridden conditions, with a limited capacity to ward off self-contempt and self-hatred, results in the possible triumph of the nihilistic threat in black America.[18]

We have been advocating what West calls "nonmarket values—love, care, service to others"—as part and parcel of the Christian contribution to ethical business, and I have argued that there is some encouragement for attempting that contribution. However, again, it seems we need to ask whether business as a cultural institution is so deeply implicated in the problems of moral decline as to be a poor candidate for reform, let alone a positive force for social change in the economic dimensions of life.

The Chicago School of economics would take a radically different position from the one our question implies and from the position that has characterized this whole discussion. For these thinkers there is no need for reform; the rational self-interest of traditional free market capitalism is already a positive force. In a new version of egoism, the Chicago School, represented by the work of Nobel laureate Gary Becker, teaches that market principles are and should be applicable of all activities of life, from family to corporation.[19]

West's analysis, in particular, gives the lie to the pretenses of the Chicago School and its followers. The impact of market values on the values of the African American community is a paradigm of what happens, as M. Douglas Meeks has put it, when "market logic" overextends itself and tries to determine the whole of life.[20]

Meeks argues that it is the role of theology to put market logic in its place and make clear that there are certain spheres of life in which it simply does not apply or work.[21] He is undoubtedly correct in his assessment. However, I want to go beyond putting market logic in its place to see whether or not the "logic" itself can be at least modified in more ethically desirable ways. I have been suggesting that there is room for positive ethical development by working toward fundamental changes in the self-understanding of business and those who work in business. This is the kind of approach taken by business ethicist Laura Nash, whose work we have discussed earlier. Nash directly attacks the egoistic, enlightened self-interest ethic of traditional business that the Chicago School seems to find so promising. In its place she offers the covenantal ethic we have already explored. This is not simply a new practical approach to ethical decision making, although there is much practical in her proposals. Rather, the covenantal ethic is a different way for business to understand itself and its total philosophy.[22] In terms I have used earlier, it is a move from self to service.

Although even the most ethically advanced business ethos may still need to be "put in its place" à la Meeks, the extensive influence of "market logic" that its critics have demonstrated makes it imperative that we work on the ethical formation of its "logic." In fact, Meeks himself appears to be working in that direction and expresses the hope that his work will lead to a greater degree of interaction between theologians and economists.[23]

All that we have been saying, then, about the Christian witness seems terribly relevant. In knowing who we are, in seeing occupation within vocation, in moving from self to service, and in the dialogical struggle to find common ground with others for seeking those values that we know are God's promise for the world's future we "leaven the lump." Our witness contributes to the shaping of our culture's ethos and the world of business that is so much a part of our culture.

To be sure, this effort will sometimes seem like spitting into the wind. We will be tempted to believe that the culture of business and economic life is so fundamentally corrupt that only prophetic rage and condemnation are appropriate, and any message of hope belongs somewhere else. Adopting a new attitude and a new management style with improved communications, establishing a system that rewards honesty, and keeping faith with all stakeholders, although ethically significant, seem hardly to make a dent in the amount of change needed. Even the larger moves we make as a society to legislate change—like affirmative action or the Clean Air Act—sometimes do not seem to make that much of a difference.

Such assessments have a basis in reality and cannot be dismissed. The earth suffers from exploitation, not from lack of adequate scientific guidance or legislative initiatives. It suffers because our thirst for its goods is unquenchable, and our willingness to accept limits has yet to be fully developed. Sexual harassment is rampant in many workplaces, not because of unclear policies and the lack of legal sanctions, but because, from our earliest youth, relations between males and females are distorted in unhealthy ways by cultural conventions that have institutionalized predatory attitudes among males. Discrimination continues unabated, not for lack of defining the rights of all people and refining the laws that protect them, but because of our alienation from one another and our tribalistic instincts for exclusion. The gap between the haves and the have-nots grows wider, globally and nationally, not for lack of economic growth, but because greed is still an enduring human trait, and prosperity therefore breeds disparity.

In sum, we do not care for the earth because we do not consistently love nature, and we do not care for each other because we do not always love one another.

Christian realism matches worldly realism point for point. Indeed, the Christian understanding of the human situation is often more profoundly realistic than many secular accounts. We recognize that, ultimately, a radical transformation of the human spirit is required if the values to which we aspire are ever to be genuinely realized.

The "really real" is that such a transformation is our genuine hope. That is, of course, the gospel promise of God's future dominion. In that dominion all things will be radically transformed; that is the promise we live by now: "if anyone is in Christ, there is a new creation: everything old has passed away; see, everything has become new!" (2 Cor. 5:17).

The present and future promise of God's reign, God's new creation in Christ, is our bulwark against moral cynicism and discouragement as we struggle for whatever gains we can make. All the penultimate, day-to-day moments of caring and service—of going beyond the moral minimum, beyond excellence to virtue, beyond affirmative action to true community, beyond mere survival to care for the earth, and beyond complacent certainty to the embrace of faith—bear witness to that radical, ultimate promise.

NOTES

1. BRIDGING THE SHAREABILITY GAP

1. James W. Kuhn and Donald W. Shriver Jr., *Beyond Success: Corporations and Their Critics in the 1990s* (Ruffin Series in Business Ethics; New York: Oxford Univ. Press, 1991), 3.

2. Ibid., 3-4.

3. *Corporate Ethics: A Prime Business Asset* (New York: Business Roundtable, 1988), 4.

4. Ibid., 9.

5. Ibid.

6. Lyle F. Schoenfeldt, Don M. McDonald, and Stuart A. Youngblood, "The Teaching of Business Ethics: A Survey of AACSB Member Schools," *Journal of Business Ethics* 10 (1992): 237-41.

7. Frida Kerner Furman, "Teaching Business Ethics: Questioning the Assumptions, Seeking New Directions," *Journal of Business Ethics* 9 (1990): 31-38.

8. Charles S. McCoy, *Management of Values* (Boston: Pitman, 1985), 61.

9. Kuhn and Shriver, *Beyond Success,* 304-5.

10. Anne Wilson Schaef, *Women's Reality* (Minneapolis: Winston Press, 1981).

11. Carol Gilligan, *In a Different Voice* (Cambridge, Mass.: Harvard Univ. Press, 1982).

12. Eric Mount Jr., *Professional Ethics in Context* (Louisville, Ky.: Westminster/John Knox Press, 1990), 54-55.

13. Laura L. Nash, *Good Intentions Aside: A Manager's Guide to Resolving Ethical Problems* (Boston: Harvard Business School Press, 1991). Charles McCoy makes a similar point in his discussion of how personal and business ethics interpenetrate; see his *Management of Values,* 46.

14. Stephen Hart and David A. Krueger, "Congregations and Business Life Project: Final Report" (Center for Ethics and Corporate Policy, July 26, 1991), 32, 34.

15. William E. Diehl, *The Monday Connection* (San Francisco: HarperCollins, 1991).

16. Frederick M. Gedicks, "The Religious, the Secular, and the Antithetical," *Capital Univ. Law Review* 20 (1991): 113-45.

17. Jack Mahoney, "Christianity and Business Ethics" (paper prepared for the international conference, "Ethics of Business in a Global Economy," sponsored by the Council for Ethics in Economics, Columbus, Ohio, March 25-27, 1992).

18. Robert Jackall, *Moral Mazes: The World of Corporate Managers* (New York: Oxford Univ. Press, 1988).

19. Quoted in Diehl, *Monday Connection,* 21.

20. Hart and Krueger, "Congregations and Business Life Project," 685.

21. Diehl, *Monday Connection,* 90.

22. David A. Krueger, "Connecting Ministry with the Corporate World," *The Christian Century* 107 (May 30-June 6, 1990), 574.

23. Nash, *Good Intentions Aside,* 24.

24. Ibid.

25. Hart and Krueger, "Congregations and Business Life Project," 27.

26. Quoted in Vernard Eller, "A Voice on Vocation: The Contribution of Jacques Ellul," *Reformed Journal* 29 (1979), 19.

27. Diehl, *Monday Connection,* 48, 175.

28. McCoy, *Management of Values,* 46-47.

29. James M. Gustafson and Elmer W. Johnson, "The Corporate Leader and the Ethical Resources of Religion: A Dialogue," in Oliver Williams and John Houck, eds., *The Judeo-Christian Vision and the Modern Corporation* (Notre Dame, Ind.: Univ. of Notre Dame Press, 1982), 319.

2. FROM BEING A NOBODY TO BEING A SOMEBODY

1. Andy Rooney, "Honors for Celebrities Often Miss the Real Achievers," *Columbus Dispatch,* Nov. 12, 1991, 8A.

2. Robert Jackall, *Moral Mazes: The World of Corporate Managers* (New York: Oxford Univ. Press, 1988), 43.

3. Ibid.

4. Ibid., 41, 45.

5. Ibid., 47-61.

6. Ibid., 73-74.

7. Ibid., 52.

8. Ibid.

9. Joanne B. Ciulla, "On the Demand for Meaningful Work," *People in Corporations,* ed. George Enderle, Brenda Almond, and Antonio Argandona (Boston: Kluwer, 1991), 114.

10. Ibid., 114-16.

11. Ibid., 117.

12. Quoted in ibid., 114.

13. Jackall, *Moral Mazes,* 75.

14. *Lutheran Book of Worship* (Minneapolis: Augsburg Publ. House, 1978), 56.

15. Wolfhart Pannenberg, *What Is Man?* trans. Duane A. Priebe (Philadelphia: Fortress Press, 1970), 41-53.

16. Nelvin Vos, "To Take Life Leisurely," *Reformed Journal* 29 (1979), 15.

17. Ibid., 16.

18. Paul S. Minear, "Work and Vocation in Scripture," *Work and Vocation,* ed. with introduction by John Oliver Nelson (New York: Harper, 1954), 47-50.

19. Ibid., 49. Nicholas Wolterstorff sees the Reformation understanding of equality in vocation in much the same way: "The Reformers saw every legitimate occupation as a vocation before the face of God, each equal in nobility with the other. In God's sight farming is as noble as scholarship, cabinet-making as preaching, politics as missionary work. All have the same status before God of being obedient responses to his calling." See idem, "More on Vocation" *Reformed Journal* 29 (1979), 22.

20. Suzanne Gordon, *Prisoners of Men's Dreams* (Boston: Little, Brown & Co., 1991), 39.

21. Ibid., 41-66.

22. Martin Luther, *A Treatise on Christian Liberty,* trans. W. A. Lambert, ed. Harold J. Grimm (Philadelphia: Fortress Press, 1957), 7, 17ff., 30-31.

23. Gustaf Wingren, *Luther on Vocation,* trans. Carl C. Rasmussen (Philadelphia: Muhlenberg, 1957), 5-7, 46-47, 66ff.

24. Lee Hardy, *Fabric of This World* (Grand Rapids, Mich.: Eerdmans, 1990), 54-57.

25. Quoted in Hardy, *Fabric of This World,* 56.

26. Ibid., 67-68.

27. See James M. Childs Jr., *Faith, Formation, and Decision* (Minneapolis: Fortress Press, 1992), 21-22.

28. See *Commonweal* 26 (1989), 281.

3. THE NOT-SO-SECULAR WORLD

1. This is from the unofficial translation of the address by Vaclav Havel, delivered at the annual meeting of the World Economic Forum in Davos on Tuesday February 4, 1992. The official translation is in preparation.

2. Carl E. Braaten, *Christ and Counter-Christ* (Philadelphia: Fortress Press, 1972), 69.

3. Havel, World Economic Forum.

4. Ibid.

5. Ibid.

6. Ibid.

7. Alasdair MacIntyre, *After Virtue* (Notre Dame, Ind.: Univ. of Notre Dame Press, 1981), 6-7.

8. Ibid., 11-12.

9. Ibid., 22-34.

10. Ibid., 24-26.

11. James W. Kuhn and Donald W. Schriver Jr., *Beyond Success: Corporations and Their Critics in the 1990s* (Ruffin Series in Business Ethics; New York: Oxford Univ. Press, 1991), 266.

12. *What You Should Know about Business Ethics,* ed. Paul Hencke (New York: Inst. of Business Management, 1987), 69-78.

13. MacIntyre, *After Virtue,* 52.

14. Ronald F. Thiemann, *Constructing a Public Theology* (Louisville, Ky.: Westminster/John Knox Press, 1991), 48.

15. Ibid., 47.

16. H. Tristram Englehart Jr., "Fashioning an Ethic for Life and Death in a Post-Modern Society, *Hastings Center Report,* 19 (1989), 8-9.

17. Thomas Donaldson, *The Ethics of International Business* (New York: Oxford Univ. Press, 1989), 10-29.

18. Ibid. 44-64.

19. Hans Küng, *Global Responsibility* (New York: Crossroad Publ. Co., 1991), 51-52.

20. Ibid., 53.

21. "America's Holy War," *Time,* 138 (1991): 68, emphasis mine.

22. Thiemann, *Public Theology,* 17.

23. Ibid.

24. Ibid., 19-20.

25. Ibid., 90-91.

26. Ibid., 38.

27. Laura L. Nash, *Good Intentions Aside: A Manager's Guide to Resolving Ethical Problems* (Boston: Harvard Business School Press, 1991). Charles McCoy makes a similar point in his discussion of how personal and business ethics interpenetrate; see his *Management of Values* (Boston: Pitman, 1985), 78.

28. Bruce Vawter, "The Gospel according to John," in Raymond E. Brown et.al., eds., *Jerome Biblical Commentary* (Englewood Cliffs, N.J.: Prentice-Hall, 1968), 469.

4. FROM DUALISM TO DIALOGUE

1. Frank K. Sonnenberg and Beverly Goldberg, "Business Integrity: An Oxymoron?" *Industry Week,* April 6, 1992, 53.

2. "Where Have Our Ethics Gone?" *Industry Week,* Sept. 16, 1991, 20.

3. Michael J. Perry, *Love and Power* (New York: Oxford Univ. Press, 1991), 8.

4. Ibid., 11-12.

5. Ibid., 29.

6. Ibid., 89.

7. Ibid., 87.

8. Ibid., 41.

9. Ibid., 100.

10. Ibid., 101.

11. Paul Tillich, "The Protestant Principle and the Proletarian Situation," *The Protestant Era,* trans. James Luther Adams (Chicago: Univ. of Chicago Press, 1957), 166-67.

12. James M. Childs Jr., "Religion and Politics: Tradition and the Post-Modern Agenda," *Capital Univ. Law Review* 20 (1991), 154-57.

13. Perry, *Love and Power,* 15.

14. M. Douglas Meeks, *God the Economist: The Doctrine of God and Political Economy* (Minneapolis: Fortress Press, 1989), 3.

15. Ibid., 47-48.

16. My first book, *Christian Anthropology and Ethics* (Philadelphia: Fortress Press, 1978), was devoted in large measure to dealing with phenomenon of dualism in Christian anthropology and its influence on the social and ethical outlook of the church.

17. Gustaf Wingren, *Lutheran Vocation,* trans. Carl C. Rasmussen (Philadelphia: Muhlenberg, 1957), 6-7; and Paul S. Minear, "Work and Vocation in Scripture," *Work and Vocation,* ed. with introduction by John Oliver Nelson (New York: Harper, 1954), 44-46.

18. I am grateful to Dennis McCann for some catalytic thoughts about the theology of economic institutions in his unpublished paper for the University of Notre Dame Center for Ethics and Religious Values in Business, "Toward a Theology of the Corporation: A Second Chance for Catholic Social Thought."

19. Luther, "Temporal Authority: To What Extent It Should Be Obeyed," in Walther I. Brandt, ed., *Luther's Works,* vol. 45 (Philadelphia: Muhlenberg Press, 1962), passim.

20. Wingren, *Luther on Vocation,* 27.

21. Ibid., 46.

22. See, e.g., Rom. 8:19-23; also the comprehensive hope for the messianic age of the future in Isa. 11:1-9.

23. Helmut Thielicke, *Theological Ethics* 1, ed. William H. Lazareth (Philadelphia: Fortress Press, 1966), 439-40.

24. "If God and economy are inextricably connected, we shall have to go against the modern stream by holding that economy is political....We are not supporting the liberal separation of politics and economy, the one public and the other private....Politics and the economy are necessary to each other...." Meeks, *God the Economist,* 6-7.

25. Remarks delivered in a panel presentation at the March 25-27, 1992, conference, "Ethics of Business in a Global Economy," sponsored by the Council for Ethics in Economics, Columbus, Ohio.

26. Meeks, *God the Economist,* 18.

27. My fuller account of this dialog with Ross Laboratories was originally presented in a paper to the Society of Christian Ethics in January 1981 and subsequently published under the title, "Dialogue with Ross Laboratories: A Chapter in the Infant Formula Controversy," *Trinity Seminary Review* 4 (1982), 3-18. Paul Minus, the leader of our church group, sounded the call for dialog in this controversy in an article in *The Christian Century,* June 20-27, 1979, "The Infant Formula Issue: Other Perspectives." The Ross dialog, then, helped to set the pattern for the United Methodist Church task force on the formula issue, of which Minus was a part.

5. Beyond the Moral Minimum

1. Jeffrey M. Kaplan, "Sentencing Guidelines: An 'Unprecedented Offer' from Government," *Ethikos* (1992), 13.

2. Robert Guelich, *The Sermon on the Mount* (Waco, Tex.: Word Books, 1982), 82- 83.

3. Tom L. Beauchamp and James F. Childress, *Principles of Biomedical Ethics* (New York: Oxford Univ. Press, 1979), 97. Although their book focuses on issues of bioethics, the authors also provide an extensive discussion of the general normative issues of ethics.

4. Richard T. De George, *Business Ethics,* 3rd ed. (New York: Macmillan, 1990), 181.

5. Ibid., 97-101.

6. Victor Paul Furnish, *The Love Command in the New Testament* (New York City: Abingdon, 1972), 51, emphasis added.

7. Guelich, *Sermon on the Mount,* 254.

8. Furnish, *Love Command,* 60-61.

9. Ibid., 41, 44-45.

10. Guelich, *Sermon on the Mount,* 263ff.

11. Beauchamp and Childress, *Principles of Biomedical Ethics,* 136.

12. Ibid., 230.

13. Helmut Thielicke's helpful discussion of the distinction between theological ethics and philosophical underscores the idea that the Christian ethic begins with God's gracious initiative, rather than focusing on our ability to do the ethical task. *Theological Ethics* 1, ed. William H. Lazareth (Philadelphia: Fortress Press, 1966), 51-52.

14. My brief comments, confined to the relation of love to beneficence in business ethics, echo Reinhold Niebuhr's understanding of the relation of love to political life and justice. See *Reinhold Niebuhr on*

Politics, ed. Harry R. Davis and Robert C. Good (New York: Scribner's, 1960), 154ff.

15. De George, *Business Ethics,* 37.

16. David L. Kirp, "Uncommon Decency: Pacific Bell Responds to AIDS," *Harvard Business Review* 89 (1989): 149.

17. Ibid., 142.

18. Ibid., 144.

19. Ibid., 141, 143.

20. Ibid., 143, 151.

21. Ibid., 145-148.

22. Ibid., passim.

23. Laura L. Nash, *Good Intentions Aside: A Manager's Guide to Resolving Ethical Problems* (Boston: Harvard Business School Press, 1991), 88-95.

24. Ibid., 95-103.

25. Ibid., 98.

26. Ibid., 110.

27. Ibid., 103-14.

28. Ibid., 83-87.

29. Joseph L. Allen, *Love and Conflict* (Nashville: Abingdon, 1984), 61.

30. Ibid., 39-40, 74-81.

31. Ibid., 41-42.

32. Ibid., 42-45.

33. Ibid., 120ff.

6. BEYOND LEADERSHIP TO SERVANT LEADERSHIP

1. *What You Should Know about Business Ethics,* Paul Hencke, ed.-in-chief (New York: National Inst. of Business Management, 1987), 7-8.

2. This emphasis on character or the virtues that comprise character is the ultimate thrust of MacIntyre's *After Virtue* (Notre Dame, Ind.: Univ. of Notre Dame Press, 1981), 210-45.

3. Charles E. Watson, *Managing with Integrity* (New York: Praeger, 1991), xiv.

4. Ibid., xv.

5. The "story-formed" character of communities and its importance for the foundation of ethics and Christian ethics have been developed most extensively by Stanley Hauerwas. See especially his book, *A Community of Character* (Notre Dame, Ind.: Univ. of Notre Dame Press, 1981). Also important is his earlier essay with David B. Burrell, "From System to Story: An Alternative Pattern for Rationality in Ethics," *Truthfulness and Tragedy* (Notre Dame, Ind.: Univ. of Notre Dame Press, 1977), 15-39.

6. From the Foreword by James O'Toole to Max De Pree, *Leadership*

Is an Art (New York: Dell Publishing, 1989), xi-xxiv.

7. See *Inc.,* 13 (July 1991), 31-32.

8. Laura L. Nash, *Good Intentions Aside: A Manager's Guide to Resolving Ethical Problems* (Boston: Harvard Business School Press, 1991). See also Charles McCoy, *Management of Values* (Boston: Putman, 1985), 19.

9. De Pree, *Leadership,* 1.

10. Ibid., 9-10.

11. Ibid., 63.

12. Ibid., 36-40.

13. Ibid., 42.

14. Ibid., 11-22.

15. Craig Cox and Sally Power, "Executive Pay: How Much Is Too Much?" *Business Ethics* 5 (1991), 18.

16. Ibid., 20.

17. Ibid., 19.

18. Ibid., 21.

19. *Theological Dictionary of the New Testament* 2, Gerhard Kittel, ed., Geoffrey Bromily, trans. and ed. (Grand Rapids, Mich.: Eerdman's, 1964), 82-83.

20. "Taking Care of Business," *Hard Choices* 1 (Fall 1991), 5.

21. Watson, *Managing with Integrity,* 251.

22. Mike Royko, "Tax Dollars Flow to Roamin' Romeo and His Seraglio," *Columbus Dispatch,* July 19, 1992, 3D.

23. Warren Bennis and Burt Nanus, *Leaders* (New York: Harper and Row, 1985), 21.

24. Ibid., 21-22.

25. Ibid., 92-93.

26. Ibid., 64.

27. Ibid., 110-51.

28. Ibid., 153.

29. James A. Waters, "Catch 20.5: Corporate Morality as an Organizational Phenomenon," in A. Pablo Iannone, ed., *Contemporary Moral Controversies in Business* (New York: Oxford Univ. Press, 1989), 153-54. Waters presents an analysis of seven different organizational models and how they help or hinder the probing, conversational, or dialogical engagement needed to make ethical consciousness an integral part of decisionmaking in general.

30. Dave Zielinski, "The Hidden Human Costs of Total Quality," *Business Ethics* 6 (1992): 24-27.

31. De Pree, *Leadership,* 90.

32. Ibid., 82.

33. Ibid., 27-29; 60-65.

34. Robert Howard, "Values Make the Company: An Interview with

Robert Haas," *Harvard Business Review* 90 (1990): 133-44.

35. Ibid., 134-135. See also my chapter on autonomy in *Faith, Formation, and Decision* (Minneapolis: Fortress Press, 1992).

36. Howard, "Values Make the Company,"135.

37. Ibid.

38. Ibid., 139.

39. Ibid., 138.

40. Kenneth E. Goodpaster and John B. Matthews Jr., "Can a Corporation Have a Conscience?" in Iannone, ed., *Contemporary Moral Controversies in Business*, 125.

41. Ibid., 126.

42. Ibid., 128-29.

43. Ibid., 126-30.

44. Ibid., 131.

7. BEYOND AFFIRMATIVE ACTION

1. Thomas B. Edsall, "The Disguised Debate for America's White Vote," *Washington Post National Weekly Edition*, 1992, 13.

2. *Columbus Dispatch*, October 22, 1991, 1D.

3. Joe Blundo, "Black Loan Applicants Rejected Twice as Often," *Columbus Dispatch*, November 11, 1992, 1G.

4. Lynne Duke, "Just When You Thought It Was the 20th Century," *Washington Post National Weekly Edition*, 1992, 37.

5. Jonathan Kozol, *Savage Inequalities* (New York: Crown Publishers, 1991), 74.

6. David H. Swinton, "Racism Is Responsible for Black Poverty," in William Dudley and Charles Cozic, eds., *Racism in America: Opposing Viewpoints* (San Diego: Greenhaven Press, 1991), 78.

7. Ibid., 80.

8. Frederick D. Sturdivant and Heidi Vernon-Wortzel, *Business and Society: A Managerial Approach*, 4th ed. (Boston: Irwin, 1992), 239-40.

9. Ibid., 240-41.

10. Ibid., 241-43.

11. Ibid., 244.

12. Ibid.

13. Benjamin L. Hooks, "Affirmative Action Benefits Minorities," in Dudley and Cozic, eds., *Racism in America: Opposing Viewpoints*, 128-32.

14. See "In Black and White," *New Republic*, June 10, 1991, 7-8; compare Priscilla Painton, "Quota Quagmire," and Sylvester Monroe, "Does Affirmative Action Help or Hurt?" in *Time*, May 27, 1991, 20-23. See also Sturdivant and Vernon-Wortzel, *Business and Society*, 249, for discussion of the 1983 Labor Department study showing the effectiveness of affirmative action.

15. Shelby Steele, "Affirmative Action Hurts Minorities," in Dudley and Cozic, eds., *Racism in America: Opposing Viewpoints,* 136.

16. Reinhold Niebuhr, *Love and Justice: Selections from the Shorter Writings of Reinhold Niebuhr,* D. B. Robertson, ed. (Louisville, Ky.: Westminster/John Knox, 1992), 25-29.

17. Sturdivant and Vernon-Wortzel, *Business and Society,* 249.

18. William A. Henry III, "Beyond the Melting Pot," *Time,* April 9, 1990, 28.

19. R. Roosevelt Thomas Jr., "From Affirmative Action to Affirming Diversity, *Harvard Business Review* 90 (1990): 107-17. See also the article on Thomas' program, "Will Diversity = Opportunity + Advancement for Blacks?" by Sheryl Hilliard Tucker and Kevin D. Thompson in *Black Enterprise* 21 (1990): 50-60.

20. Ibid., 109.

21. Ibid., 112.

22. Ibid., 114.

23. See James M. Childs Jr., *Christian Anthropology and Ethics* (Philadelphia: Fortress Press, 1978), especially 99ff.

24. Thomas, "Affirmative Action," 113-14.

25. Cornel West, *Race Matters* (Boston: Beacon Press, 1993), 63-67.

26. Ibid.

27. D'Vera Cohn and Barbara Vobejda, "When Blue Collar Jobs Are a Barrier," *Washington Post National Weekly Edition,* December 18, 1992-January 3, 1993, 32.

28. I. Devine and D. Markiewicz, "Cross-Sex Relationships at Work and the Impact of Gender Stereotypes, *Journal of Business Ethics* 9 (1990), 333.

29. Ibid.

30. Karen Korabik, "Androgyny and Leadership Style," *Journal of Business Ethics* 9 (1990), 285.

31. Suzanne Gordon, *Prisoners of Men's Dreams* (Boston: Little, Brown & Co., 1991), 24-25.

32. Ibid., 26.

33. Ibid., 274-75.

34. Ibid., 286-87, 275.

35. Korabik, "Androgyny and Leadership Style," 288.

36. James Nelson, *The Intimate Connection* (Philadelphia: Westminster, 1988), 97.

8. BEYOND MERE SURVIVAL

1. Hans Küng, *Global Responsibility* (New York: Crossroad Publ. Co., 1991), 29-31.

2. E. S. Woolard, "Corporate Environmentalism," unpublished remarks for the Ariel Halpern Memorial Symposium on Business Ethics, Dartmouth College, Hanover, New Hampshire, November 21, 1991.

3. H. Paul Santmire, *The Travail of Nature* (Philadelphia: Fortress Press, 1985), ch. 1.

4. Ibid., passim.

5. James A. Nash, *Loving Nature* (Nashville: Abingdon, 1991), 68-92.

6. Santmire, *Travail,* 127.

7. Ibid., 131.

8. Ibid., 133-35.

9. Ibid., 135-40. Santmire cites Albrecht Ritschl, Wilhelm Herrmann, Søren Kierkegaard, Rudolf Bultmann, and Emil Brunner as leaders in the strong anthropocentric focus of mainstream theological scholarship.

10. "The North-South Connection...Sustainable Development Broadens Its Horizon," *Conservation Exchange* 10 (1992), 1, 6-7.

11. Thomas N. Gladwin, *Building the Sustainable Corporation* (Washington, D.C.: National Wildlife Federation Corporate Conservation Council, 1992), esp. 19ff.

12. Stephen Schmidheiny and Lloyd Timberlake, *Changing Course: A Global Business Perspective on Development and the Environment* (Cambridge, Mass.: M.I.T. Press, 1992), 11.

13. W. Michael Hoffman, "Business and Environmental Ethics," *Business Ethics Quarterly* 1 (1991), 170-72.

14. Ibid., 172-73.

15. Ibid., 176.

16. Schmidheiny and Timberlake, *Changing Course,* 107.

17. Matt. 7:24-27.

18. Robert Guelich, *The Sermon on the Mount* (Waco, Tex.: Word Books, 1982), 411-13.

19. Hoffman, "Business and Environmental Ethics," 177-82.

20. Eugene C. Hargrove, *Foundations of Environmental Ethics* (Englewood Cliffs, N.J.: Prentice-Hall, 1989), 104.

21. Ibid., 48-104. Hargrove finds resources for grounding the intrinsic value of nature in a variety of places: Lewis and Clark, the aesthetics of G. E. Moore, nineteenth-century environmentalism, the enormously influential work of Aldo Leopold, and the philosophy of Alfred North Whitehead, to cite a few prominent examples.

22. Holmes Rolston, III, *Environmental Ethics* (Philadelphia: Temple Univ. Press, 1988), see esp. chs. 6 and 8.

23. Hargrove, *Foundations,* 15.

24. Gladwin, *Building the Sustainable Corporation,* 19, emphasis mine.

25. Compare Nash, *Loving Nature,* 106-7.

26. Santmire, *Travail*, 197.

27. Ibid., 200-208; Nash, *Loving Nature*, 124-33; James M. Childs Jr., *Faith, Formation, and Decision* (Minneapolis: Fortress Press, 1992), 15-18.

28. These remarks and those in the next section were developed during my work on the Evangelical Lutheran Church in America's task force for the development of the church social statement, "Caring for Creation: Vision, Hope, and Justice," which was adopted at the 1993 church-wide assembly. My language and insight here were strongly influenced by my colleagues on the task force, particularly Paul Santmire and Robert Stivers, who represented the Presbyterian Church (USA).

29. *Restoring Creation for Ecology and Justice*, A Report Adopted by the 202nd General Assembly (1990) Presbyterian Church (USA) (Louisville, Ky.: Office of the General Assembly PCUSA, 1990), 23.

30. Schmidheiny and Timberlake, *Changing Course*, 11-12. See also the discussion of long-term partnerships, 127ff.

31. William Diehl, *The Monday Connection* (San Francisco: HarperCollins, 1991), 156ff.

32. Schmidheiny and Timberlake, *Changing Course*, 127ff.

33. Ibid., 221-22.

34. Ibid., 16-18.

35. Nash, *Loving Nature*, 63-67.

36. Quoted in Ronald Cole-Turner, *The New Genesis* (Louisville, Ky.: Westminster/John Knox Press, 1993), 10-11.

9. BEYOND CERTAINTY

1. Andrew Stark, "What's the Matter with Business Ethics?" *Harvard Business Review* 93 (1993), 38.

2. Laura L. Nash, *Good Intentions Aside: A Manager's Guide to Resolving Ethical Problems* (Boston: Harvard Business School Press, 1991). See also Charles McCoy, *Management of Values* (Boston: Pitman, 1985), 124-26.

3. *In This Case: Case Studies in Business Ethics* (Louisville, Ky.: Presbyterian Publishing House, 1993), 27-29.

4. Helmut Thielicke, *Theological Ethics* 1, ed. William H. Lazareth (Philadelphia: Fortress Press, 1966), 95-96.

5. James M. Childs Jr., *Faith, Formation, and Decision* (Philadelphia: Fortress Press, 1992), 93-95.

6. A recent and notable study on justice in the workplace is Blair H. Sheppard, Roy J. Lewicki, and John W. Minton, *Organized Justice* (New York: Lexington Books, 1992).

7. Michael Rion, *The Responsible Manager* (San Francisco: Harper and Row, 1990), 26-30.

8. Ibid., 13-14. Parenthetical comments mine.

9. Laura Nash, *Good Intentions Aside,* 160 and 86.

10. Ibid., 130.

11. Childs, *Faith, Formation, and Decision,* 120-21.

12. James A. Nash, *Loving Nature* (Nashville: Abingdon, 1991), 186-91.

13. "Code of Ethics," a pamphlet published by the American Society of CLU and CHFC, Bryn Mawr, Penn., n.d.

14. See "Corporate Ethics Practices," the Conference Board, Report Number 986, 1992, 34.

15. Darrel Rowland, "Whistle-Blowers Face Risks, Costly Retaliation," *Columbus Dispatch,* January 26, 1992, 4E.

16. "Poor Health Is Often the Price of Courage," *Columbus Dispatch,* January 26, 1992, 5E.

17. "Is Whistle-Blowing the Same as Informing?" *Contemporary Moral Controversies in Business,* ed. A. Pablo Iannone (New York: Oxford Univ. Press, 1989), 207.

18. Ibid., 207-20.

19. Michael G. Bowen and F. Clark Power, "The Moral Manager: Communicative Ethics and the *Exxon Valdez* Disaster," *Business Ethics Quarterly Review* 3 (1993), 97-115.

20. Ibid., 97-103.

21. Ibid., 104-07.

10. BEYOND THE COMPANY WALLS

1. See *Apology of the Augsburg Confession,* XVIII, 4-5, as an example of the "civil righteousness" of basic morality that people are to some extent capable of achieving by reason and free will. See also the discussion of "Natural Law" in James F. Childress and John Macquarrie, eds., *The Westminster Dictionary of Christian Ethics,* (Philadelphia: Westminster, 1986).

2. Daniel Maguire, T*he Moral Core of Judaism and Christianity: Reclaiming the Revolution* (Minneapolis: Fortress Press, 1993), 50, 53. Maguire is citing work of Elaine Pagels and Gary Wills in these comments.

3. See Michael G. Bowen and F. Clark Power, "The Moral Manager: Communicative Ethics and the *Exxon Valdez* Disaster," *Business Ethics Quarterly Review* 3 (1993), 116-67.

4. Stephen Schmidheiny and Lloyd Timberlake, *Changing Course* (Cambridge, Mass.: M.I.T. Press, 1992), 86. Emphasis mine.

5. *On the Road to Success,* Responsible Care Progress Report 1992-1993, Chemical Manufacturer's Association, 35.

6. This remark is based on informal conversations with environmen-

talists and others reviewing and evaluating responsible care at a Council for Ethics in Economics planning conference in Chicago, September 2-3, 1993.

7. *Annual Report,* Council for Ethics in Economics, Columbus, Ohio, 1993, 10.

8. The proceedings of the conference are published in *The Ethics of Business in a Global Economy,* ed. Paul M. Minus (Boston: Kluwer Academic Publishers, 1993).

9. See ibid., 44-45.

10. Hans Küng, *Global Responsibility* (New York: Crossroad Publ. Co., 1991), 51-53.

11. Ibid., 94-105.

12. Ibid.

13. Based on conversation with Paul Minus, a task force member.

14. "Responsible Care," Harvard Business School Case N9-391-135 prepared by Jeffrey F. Rappaport and George C. Lodge (1991), 5-7.

15. Larry L. Rasmussen, *Moral Fragments and Moral Community* (Minneapolis: Fortress Press, 1993), 106.

16. Ibid., 41-68 and passim.

17. Cornel West, *Race Matters* (Boston: Beacon Press, 1993), 16-17.

18. Ibid., 17.

19. Rasmussen, *Moral Fragments,* 48-50.

20. M. Douglas Meeks, *God the Economist: The Doctrine of God and Political Economy* (Minneapolis: Fortress Press, 1989), 37-39.

21. Ibid.

22. Laura L. Nash, *Good Intentions Aside: A Manager's Guide to Resolving Ethical Problems* (Boston: Harvard Business School Press, 1991).

23. Meeks, *God the Economist,* xii.

INDEX